Boris v. Ken

How Boris Johnson Won London

In memory of Gareth Butler,
who loved elections

Boris v. Ken

How Boris Johnson Won London

Giles Edwards and Jonathan Isaby

POLITICO'S

First published in Great Britain 2008 by
Politico's Publishing, an imprint of
Methuen Publishing Ltd
8 Artillery Row
London
SW1P 1RZ

10 9 8 7 6 5 4 3 2 1

A CIP catalogue record for this book is available from the British Library.

ISBN 978-1-84275-225-8

Set in Garamond and Futura by Methuen Publishing Ltd
Printed and bound in Great Britain by CPD Wales, Blaina

Contents

Introduction

When Boris Johnson was first mentioned in July 2007 as a possible candidate for Mayor of London, the prospect of him running – let alone winning – was considered so bizarre that the BBC's political editor, Nick Robinson, who had got the tip-off, didn't press to get it on the main evening news. Two weeks later, when Boris cycled across to City Hall and confirmed that he was indeed running, the event was so chaotic that some wondered how seriously he intended taking the election. His team initially found him frustrating to work with, and the man himself found it hard to express why he wanted to be Mayor. Yet just ten months after Robinson's exclusive, more than 1.1 million people voted for Boris. He defeated Ken Livingstone, the incumbent Mayor and a man who had seen off attempts by both Margaret Thatcher and Tony Blair to end his political career. Even on the morning of his triumph many Londoners, when told Ken looked likely to lose, were asking: 'Are you serious?' How on earth did Boris do it?

This book tells that story – how Boris won London. Who helped him? Who tried to hurt him? And what of the others involved – the journalists, the commentators, the candidates for the smaller parties – and their sometimes outsized characters? But most of all it tells the story of what happened when Ken and Boris – two politicians known throughout the country by their first names alone – came head to head.

In one sense the election was just a battle over who could get their vote out on the day. A study by Marc Williams of the BBC's political research unit showed that if all the people who had voted for the Conservatives in the 2006 borough elections did so again on 1 May, Boris would become Mayor. If he could get people who had already voted Conservative within the last two years – particularly in the outer London boroughs – to do so again, he didn't need to persuade a single new person to vote Conservative. This was the core of the Conservative strategy, but whilst it may have been based on a simple premise, making it work would not be easy. Boris needed to persuade those recent Conservative voters that they shouldn't let the other guy win by default; he needed to persuade them that he could win; and he needed to persuade them that that would be a good thing. He needed to do all of this against a tricky and incredibly experienced politician who knew the city intimately. So whilst turnout mattered, there was a lot more to it than that. Fortunately he had some considerable strengths of his own. Boris Johnson was an extremely strong brand. Funny, buffoonish, quick witted, he was incredibly well known and well liked. This was vital in so many ways, not least as he faced charges that he was a racist: they just didn't square with people's impression of Boris.

For Ken, because Boris was his right-wing mirror image, this was, as he acknowledged, the most formidable challenge he had ever faced. Ken was the incumbent, and with eight years of experience in the office he could no longer compete with Boris for the wow factor, and he had to find a new routine. His campaign focused on competence, the argument that he had done a good job of running London, that the city was a better place because of him, and that Boris would jeopardise its success and prosperity. His experience would stand in sharp contrast to Boris's inexperience and the apparent chaos of his personal and political lives.

The danger for Ken was that if someone could show he wasn't very competent – that London hadn't been very well run – this narrative would start to unravel, and that is where the drama's third major player came in. He was neither candidate, campaign manager nor activist, but a journalist who just a few years before had left his job after the death of a source and one of the greatest editorial crises in BBC history. Andrew Gilligan had resurfaced at the *Evening Standard* and his investigative reporting – which raised serious questions about how taxpayers' money was being spent at the London Development Agency – was to be an absolutely vital part of Ken's downfall. On the day Boris became Mayor the paper even ran the headline '*Standard* investigations help to oust Ken'. Gilligan himself was rather more restrained, noting that it was as much Ken's response as the allegations themselves which did for him; and indeed the way the Mayor answered his critics was to be much more of an issue in this election than it had been four or eight years previously.

The battle between Boris and Ken was not just about London, though. Politically it was also a proxy war between David Cameron and Gordon Brown. Inexperience versus experience. Youth and dynamism versus a track record. Policy vagueness versus policy slip-ups after years in power. Both party leaders had a slightly awkward relationship with their candidate, yet both needed him to win as an important staging post on their own political journeys. Boris's victory now gives the Conservatives a chance to use London as a laboratory in which they can pilot their ideas and pet projects. There are huge benefits to that but, of course, huge risks. If things go wrong, Labour will be able to point at London and say: 'Do you really want that for the whole country?'

And then there were the others, although so squeezed out that none received more than 10 per cent of the final vote. The squeeze was exacerbated by the media devoting most of its attention to the fight between the two men who could be Mayor, Boris and Ken.

Worst hit was the Liberal Democrat, Brian Paddick, who found the campaign an enormously frustrating experience. Was it inevitable that in a campaign where two candidates went only by their first names the others should be marginalised? Whatever the answer to that question, we have chosen in this book to reflect reality and refer throughout to 'Boris' and 'Ken'.

What is certain is that Boris, Ken and all the other candidates, with their personal foibles and quirks, have made this book tremendous fun to write. For all their occasional mutterings about some other camp's skulduggery we, and many Londoners, have enjoyed watching them go at it. They have enlivened the political process – and an extra half-million Londoners went out to vote as a result. We would like to thank them for that.

Some other, more personal thanks are also in order. First to all those on the various campaigns, and among London's fine journalist corps, who shared their time and thoughts with us. To our publishers, Politico's, where the idea first sprang from Alan Gordon Walker's fertile mind and where Jonathan Wadman has laboured long and hard to smooth out the manuscript. To our agent, Nicola Barr, for demystifying the process for one of us and introducing an element of calm for the other. Giles would like to thank Sue Inglish, Gavin Allen, Jo Carr, Peter Snowdon, David Cowling, Karl Mercer, Rebecca Towers and all his friends and colleagues at the BBC for their help and forbearance. He has a debt, too, to Andy Holliday, but above all he would like to thank Vinita for her love and support, and for putting up with long hours spent typing in front of an ever-expanding series of new gadgets. Jonathan would like to thank Will Lewis and Iain Martin at the *Daily Telegraph*, as well as the many other colleagues and friends who have given advice and encouragement. He would also like to apologise to the friends and family he has neglected during the course of writing the book, but most of all he wants to thank

Claudia for all her love, support and understanding throughout. For all that these others have helped the final responsibility lies, as ever, with us, and any errors or omissions which remain are ours, and ours alone.

One final note. Our wonderful friend Gareth Butler died, well before his time, earlier this year. Gareth loved elections: he was raised on an election-rich diet and was the BBC's editor of radio election programmes for five years. It seemed appropriate to dedicate this book to his memory.

The beginnings of the London mayoralty

London elected its first Mayor on 4 May 2000, just over four years after the idea was proposed in a consultation document, *A Voice for London*, published by the Labour Party in opposition.

Michael Heseltine, Deputy Prime Minister for the final couple of years of John Major's Government, had been keen on the idea of directly elected executive mayors, but was unable to persuade Major to adopt the policy. Yet by that stage, the Conservatives were staring an almost inevitable general election defeat in the face and a rejuvenated Labour Party under Tony Blair was heading for its first election victory in over two decades. So when Blair, riding high in the opinion polls, pledged to recreate a strategic London authority, the first seed was sown of an office which would give one individual a greater direct electoral mandate than any other politician in Britain.

Ironically enough, Frank Dobson, the environment spokesman in Blair's Shadow Cabinet and later the party's official mayoral candidate in 2000, was lukewarm to the idea of an elected Mayor. However, Blair, never one to be coy about overriding internal opposition, pressed ahead and the 1997 Labour manifesto reminded us that London was 'the only Western capital without an elected city government'. It continued:

> Following a referendum to confirm popular demand,
> there will be a new deal for London, with a strategic
> authority and a mayor, each directly elected. Both will
> speak up for the needs of the city and plan its future. They
> will not duplicate the work of the boroughs, but take
> responsibility for London-wide issues – economic regen-
> eration, planning, policing, transport and environmental
> protection.

Elected with its landslide majority in May 1997, the new Labour
Government set about putting its programme into effect, some
measures faster than others. In terms of constitutional changes, its
first priority was setting up the devolved bodies in Scotland and
Wales, with referendums held just four months later, in September
1997.

The Scots positively embraced the setting up of their own
Parliament, but a week later their Celtic cousins endorsed the creation
of the National Assembly for Wales by only the narrowest of margins,
on a turnout of a fraction over 50 per cent. Nonetheless, the green
light had been given for the first tranche of devolution and London
was next on the agenda.

Not that the idea of a directly elected London Mayor found
favour among all Labour MPs. The member for Brent East, one Ken
Livingstone, described the plan for a directly elected Mayor as
'absolutely barmy' in October 1997: 'I myself know only four
Labour London MPs who support this idea,' he said. 'Most others
say privately that the idea is absolutely barmy but they don't want to
rock the boat … Why would we possibly want to have a US-style
Mayor? It would be the focal point for corruption on a very large
scale.'

But more of him later.

In March 1998 a White Paper was published outlining the Government's proposals for a Mayor and Assembly in the capital, which was put to the people in a referendum on 7 May, to coincide with the four-yearly cycle of elections to the thirty-two London boroughs. Both Labour and the Liberal Democrats had supported the idea of a new strategic authority for London at the general election the previous year and polling showed that there was widespread support for – or, at least, little active hostility to – the plans put forward by the Government.

A coalition of individuals came together to form a 'Yes for London' campaign to persuade the public of the merits of a Mayor and Assembly. Many involved were putative Labour mayoral or Assembly candidates themselves and included Toby Harris, leader of Haringey Borough Council (later Lord Harris of Haringey), Barking MP Margaret Hodge and Trevor Phillips, presenter of LWT's *The London Programme*. Then there were other cheerleaders for the cause, such as the journalist Simon Jenkins and the TV executive Greg Dyke, as well as Michael Cassidy and Judith Mayhew from the Corporation of London, the local authority for the City of London.

Except for a few maverick individuals, there was never really much organised opposition to the plans for a Mayor and Assembly: the Conservatives were still smarting from their electoral drubbing the previous year, which had left them with only eleven of the capital's seventy-four parliamentary seats after a swing to Labour which hit double figures. In the event, the official Conservative position was to be in favour of an elected Mayor but opposed to the Assembly – which was not even an option on the ballot paper in the simple all-or-nothing referendum. However, individual Tories – notably the future mayoral hopefuls Lord Archer of Weston-super-Mare and Steve Norris – did end up personally backing the 'yes' campaign.

Yet the result of the referendum was hardly a ringing endorsement.

Whilst 71 per cent of those voting backed the Mayor and Assembly – and every borough produced a 'yes' vote, as did the City – it was on a pretty derisory turnout of 34 per cent, more or less consistent with a normal local election turnout. In other words, less than a quarter of the London electorate actively went out to show their support for the devolved London-wide government which the Labour manifesto a year before had declared to be 'urgently required'.

Then began the two-year marathon which would culminate in Britain's capital city having its first-ever elected Mayor and the restoration of strategic London government for the first time since the abolition of the Greater London Council in 1986.

The first move was to bring in the legislation to set up the Greater London Authority, as the Mayor and London Assembly were to be collectively known. A bill was announced in the Queen's Speech of November 1998; once enacted it was said to be the longest single piece of legislation since the Government of India Act was passed in the 1930s. To say that it was complicated and unwieldy is something of an understatement: the original bill presented to Parliament, which passed its second reading in the Commons on 14 December 1998, ran to 277 clauses and 21 schedules across 213 pages. By the time the House of Lords had scrutinised it, a further fifty-three clauses and six schedules had been added, accounting for a further seventy-five pages. A vast number of the amendments being introduced came from the Government itself, due to drafting errors and oversights by the civil servants who had the task of ensuring the technical detail of the legislation was watertight.

The system proposed for electing the Mayor – who would have a four-year term – was a curious one called supplementary vote (SV). Under most fully proportional systems, voters get to rank as many candidates as they wish in preference order, with their vote transferring to another candidate when one is eliminated. However, SV only allows for a first and second preference to be stated. Once the first-preference votes are counted, all but the top two candidates are excluded (assuming no candidate wins more than 50 per cent), and their second preferences redistributed. However, only the second-preference votes cast for those top two candidates are counted. It is, if you like, a less democratic version of the French presidential system, where there is a run-off between the top two candidates two weeks after the first ballot in which every voter gets to indicate a preference. The system was reported to be used in only one other country in the democratic world – to elect the President of Sri Lanka – and was always going to make the mayoral election a struggle for the usually third-placed Liberal Democrats. In 2008 the effect would be that if you used either your first- or second-preference vote for Ken or Boris, your vote would affect the final result; if you didn't, it wouldn't.

Meanwhile, the mayoral candidates were to be given the challenge of raising a £10,000 deposit – only returnable if they won more than 5 per cent of the vote – as well as collecting nomination signatures from ten voters in each of the thirty-two boroughs and the City of London. This would clearly be more of a challenge for candidates from the smaller parties.

As for the twenty-five Assembly members, they would be elected through the additional member system of proportional representation, which was being used to elect the Scottish Parliament and Welsh Assembly in May 1999. Fourteen Assembly members would be elected through the traditional first-past-the-post method in individual super-constituencies – a system which was again likely to elect candidates from only the two main parties. But the remaining eleven would be assigned from party lists in order to ensure that the political make-up of the Assembly reflected the proportion of votes attained by each party across the capital as a whole. No party could win one of these 'top-up' seats on the Assembly, however, unless it won 5 per cent of the pan-London vote. That particular measure was widely believed to have been introduced as a way of stopping the British National Party gaining a foothold in the Assembly, although it also made life harder for other smaller parties. In any case, it was going to make it virtually impossible for any party to win a majority of seats on the Assembly, ensuring that consensus politics would be the order of the day.

But rules for the election made up only a small part of the legislation. There were new bodies to be established and powers to be created and transferred. A new London Fire and Emergency Planning Authority was to be set up whilst the Metropolitan Police Authority would make the city's police accountable to a body other than the Home Secretary for the first time since 1829. The London Development Agency would be there to allocate funds for inward investment and regeneration, whilst Transport for London would oversee the capital's transport system. The new Mayor would be able to make appointments to all of these bodies and would set a budget which could only be amended by a two-thirds majority on the Assembly. Further powers to raise money were to be given to the Mayor through provision for congestion charging and a tax on workplace parking spaces.

Other mayoral obligations would be to produce an annual report, organise an annual 'State of London' debate and subject him- or herself to public scrutiny at a 'People's Question Time' twice a year.

The Greater London Authority Act passed into law on 11 November 1999, by which time mayoral candidates for the Green Party and the Liberal Democrats had been in place for six and three months respectively. Darren Johnson, for the Greens, had been chosen by a ballot of his party's members in the capital and was eventually elected to the Assembly via the top-up list. Susan Kramer, for the Liberal Democrats, had also been chosen by a simple ballot of her party's members in London, through the single transferable vote system. Both Johnson and Kramer would fight the election the following May, but the only other main candidate in place at that time, the Conservatives' Lord Archer, was about to get his come-uppance. Labour, meanwhile, was only just deciding how to select its candidate.

As soon as it became clear that the job of London Mayor would be up for grabs, Archer coveted the role and openly set about securing the Conservative nomination. After a short stint on the old Greater London Council in the late 1960s, he had entered Parliament at a 1969 by-election, but had to resign when he faced bankruptcy in 1974. He quickly bounced back once he started using his storytelling abilities to make a fortune as a novelist, and reappeared on the Tory circuit as an enthusiastic campaigner and a regular after-dinner speaker. Promoted to be party deputy chairman in 1985, he then found himself resigning again a year later, when the *Daily Star* alleged that he had slept with a prostitute, although he won record damages in the resulting libel action the following year. Made a life peer in 1992, he was the kind of character for whom the job of Mayor seemed suited – a populist figurehead with a vision, if not with the necessary grasp of the detail and the small print (an accusation to be levelled at Boris Johnson eight years later).

Archer set up a website, London Forum, to showcase his plans and promote his cause, and courted the Tory faithful in London on the 'rubber chicken circuit'. Eager to demonstrate his enthusiasm for the job, he organised a week shadowing Rudy Giuliani, New York's Mayor, and would talk about his experience 'working' with him at virtually every opportunity that arose. His agenda was unashamedly populist, and he pledged to hold a 'People's Question Time' every week and to donate his salary to charity.

A number of individuals inside Conservative HQ were uncomfortable about the notion of an Archer candidacy (and subsequent mayoralty), since he had a reputation for not always telling the whole truth and a history of making unfortunate gaffes. As a result, other high-profile party figures such as Chris Patten and Gyles Brandreth were unsuccessfully approached about standing.

The only other credible heavyweight candidate who emerged on the Conservative side was Steve Norris, who had been MP for Epping Forest from 1988 to 1997 (having represented Oxford East from 1983 to 1987). His credentials were bolstered by the fact that he had latterly served as Minister for Transport in London, although – presumably sensing a period in opposition ahead – he had decided to stand down from Parliament, as he said, 'to spend more time with my money'. Norris, however, was not without controversy in his past either. During his time as a minister, he had been exposed in the press as having had a succession of mistresses, but as a media-friendly and clubbable politician who had never played the morality card, he managed to survive in office. He also had a habit of being a little too candid at times, demonstrated, for example, by his one-time defence of people's car use on the grounds that commuters were 'dreadful human beings'. A number of relatively unknown local councillors and party worthies also put in for the Conservative nomination, but after a series of party committee meetings and a hustings attended by about 1,800 activists, it inevitably came down to an Archer versus Norris contest.

Archer had pressed all the buttons he needed to with grassroots Tory audiences, talking tough on crime and boasting of support from John Major and Margaret Thatcher. He was also able to take the moral high ground as regards party loyalty, since Norris had been filmed during the latter stages of the campaign for the nomination telling a party activist that he 'wouldn't support Archer alive or dead'.

Archer beat Norris two to one in a ballot of party members in

London and his candidacy was announced on 1 October 1999. The team of advisers who had been working with him on the bid for the nomination swiftly became an embryonic mayoral campaign, but his candidacy lasted less than two months. He was forced to stand down on 20 November in advance of tabloid revelations the following day that he had asked a friend to give a false alibi during that 1987 libel trial. He was thrown out of the Conservative Party and went on to be jailed for perjury and attempting to pervert the course of justice.

An initial decision by the party's top brass immediately to install Norris as candidate was swiftly reversed and nominations were reopened for the Conservative candidacy. And despite Norris having previously weathered the media storm over his private life, party insiders were more concerned than ever after the Archer debacle that the new mayoral candidate should not be a liability. To this end, a number of individuals were (unsuccessfully) approached about throwing their hat into the ring, including Michael Heseltine, Shaun Woodward, the party's London spokesman, and the gay businessman Ivan Massow. There then followed an attempt to derail Norris's candidacy by party officers in his old constituency, who accused Norris of dishonesty. However, after a seemingly endless series of meetings, he was finally selected on 17 January 2000 after a further ballot of party members, winning an emphatic victory against former Hillingdon councillor Andrew Boff.

If the selection of a Conservative candidate was deemed to have been the political equivalent of a Whitehall farce, then Labour's travails became a long-running Westminster soap opera. Although he had initially had reservations about going for the job, Ken Livingstone – whose background is covered in more detail in his own chapter – was already publishing a personal manifesto as early in the process as August 1998. As the last leader of the Greater London Council before its abolition, he seemed uniquely qualified to head London's new strategic authority, although a man so at odds with large swathes of New Labour policy and a regular rebel against the Government was never going to be Tony Blair's favoured candidate.

But if not him, then who could Labour credibly put up? Non-party figures such as Sir Richard Branson, Michael Cassidy and the independent MP Martin Bell were all sounded out, to no avail, whilst the Labour names being thrown up included Cabinet ministers Frank Dobson and Mo Mowlam, junior Transport Minister Glenda Jackson, Sports Minister Tony Banks, Toby Harris and Trevor Phillips.

Phillips and Jackson declared their intentions to run and had the Labour machine organised a swift selection and swung in behind one of them, the eventual result may have been different, but valuable time was lost. Then along came Nick Raynsford, the Minister for London, who had steered the Greater London Authority Bill through the Commons. He announced his candidacy just after the Labour conference in September 1999, following an assurance from Dobson, the Health Secretary, that he wouldn't be standing and with warm words of encouragement from Downing Street. Yet just days later Dobson performed a spectacular U-turn and announced that he would be standing after all, leaving the Labour loyalist Raynsford to conclude that he could do nothing but step aside and support his senior ministerial colleague.

Banks appeared at the Dobson campaign launch in early October and Phillips folded his own campaign to back the Health Secretary's bid a few days later. But Jackson continued apace with her candidacy, eager that a woman should be in the frame and all the more resilient because of press speculation that she too would back down and support Dobson.

Now until this point, Labour had intended selecting its candidate through a standard one member, one vote mechanism in which any candidate nominated by one eighth of constituency Labour parties in the capital would appear on the ballot paper. But this all changed when the party's National Executive Committee proposed an electoral college, in which the votes would be divided equally among three groups: Labour MPs, MEPs and GLA candidates; the trades unions and affiliated organisations; and of course rank-and-file party members.

Most observers concluded that this was a fix to prevent Ken becoming the candidate. The logic followed that the party felt it could not get away with stopping Ken's name from appearing on the ballot paper, but at the same time it needed to minimise the chance of him winning the ballot. Further accusations of an anti-Ken stitch-up were made in the ensuing weeks. Firstly, it emerged that several unions likely to be sympathetic to the Brent East MP – including the RMT, ASLEF and the MSF – were to be barred from taking part in the ballot because they were late paying their affiliation fees to the London regional Labour Party. This was in contrast to lapsed party members, who were given time to pay up and get a vote. Secondly, unions were not going to be obliged to ballot their membership, and even if they did, votes would not have to be allocated proportionately, but on a winner-takes-all basis if the unions so desired. This meant that if Downing Street leaned hard enough on union bosses, their votes would drop into Dobson's column and not Ken's, whatever their members wanted. Thirdly, it would emerge that Dobson's campaign seemingly had gained access to party membership lists – containing vital contact details for canvassing purposes – and allegations were made that Labour HQ had broken election rules to pass them on.

There was also one final hurdle for Ken to clear: a party selection panel which needed to give the all-clear to candidates appearing on the ballot paper. It needed to meet twice before giving him the green light in mid-November, at which point he, Dobson and Jackson were deemed fit to stand for the Labour nomination.

The campaign for the nomination then went on itself for nearly three months, with Livingstone and Jackson complaining that the party machine was tacitly and unfairly working for Dobson; Jackson would announce that, for what it was worth, she was giving her own second preference to Ken. Tony Blair and Gordon Brown weighed in behind Dobson with vitriolic attacks on Ken, but Dobson himself began to realise that such assistance was actually hindering his own chances and playing into the hands of Ken, who could act the victim.

It was not until 20 February 2000, less than eleven weeks before the real election, that Labour's candidate was announced: it was to be Dobson. He had beaten Ken by a whisker – 51.5 per cent to 48.5 per cent – after Jackson's votes were redistributed. Unsurprisingly, Dobson had triumphed by a country mile among the (mainly loyalist) MPs, MEPs and GLA candidates, whilst Ken won the party members 60-40. Ken also won the popular vote in the unions' section, but the margin by which he was ahead of Dobson was reduced when votes were allocated as the unions wished them to be. Ken cried foul and invited Dobson to stand down, but Dobson refused to budge. Yet it would be another two weeks before Ken broke all the promises he had previously made about supporting whoever was the Labour candidate and declared his candidacy as an independent, and the real campaign for the mayoralty began in earnest. He did so doubtless buoyed by the knowledge that opinion polls had been stating for months that he could win without a party machine behind him.

With both major parties having provided a drama lasting months over who would be their candidates, the final eight weeks in the run-up to polling day did not provide anything like as much excitement, not least because it was looking increasingly inevitable that Ken would storm to victory. Susan Kramer for the Liberal Democrats struggled to make an impact, trailing in fourth place in the polls. Steve Norris, meanwhile, was deemed to be having a good campaign, and overtook Dobson in the polls to become the main challenger to Ken.

The Conservative candidate opposed using the mayoral powers to introduce congestion charging and had other populist policies such as opening the Tube throughout the night on Thursdays, Fridays and Saturdays and wanting to charge contractors for digging up London's streets. Dobson's manifesto also proposed some eye-catching ideas, such as a new London lottery to raise money for life-enhancing schemes in the city and giving every London resident a named local police officer. Ken, meanwhile, proceeded with his campaigns against the proposed public–private partnership for the Tube and for introducing a congestion charging scheme during his first term in office. But in the event the individuals' policies didn't count for all that much, in a contest which was dominated by competing personalities.

In the end the results bore out the pollsters' predictions, with Ken taking 39 per cent of first-preference votes, compared to Norris's 27.1 per cent. Dobson trailed in third with 13.1 per cent and Kramer was hot on his heels with 11.9 per cent. No other candidate retained their deposit and after the redistribution of second preferences, Ken had 57.9 per cent to Norris's 42.1 per cent. Turnout was only 34.3 per cent. On the new London Assembly, the Conservatives and Labour each took nine seats, the Liberal Democrats four and the Greens three, partly bolstered by the support for their Assembly list candidates from Ken himself.

The Livingstone–Norris rematch four years later, in June 2004, was something of a damp squib by comparison, with nothing like as much of the drama, party infighting, resignations and general pandemonium which enlivened the first London mayoral election.

As detailed later in the book, Ken rejoined the Labour Party in January 2004, having applied for the second time the previous month. Yet for over a year a Labour candidate for the 2004 mayoral election had technically been in place in the form of Nicky Gavron, who had beaten Tony Banks to the Labour nomination. However, polls showed Gavron, the Assembly member for Enfield & Haringey and formerly Ken's Deputy Mayor, trailing in fourth place behind the Liberal Democrats if Ken stood as an independent. In the event, when Ken was readmitted to the party she fell on her sword, leaving the way clear for the incumbent Mayor to be adopted as the Labour candidate. This occurred after a ballot of London Labour members and affiliates which gave him an endorsement of nearly 94 per cent.

For the Conservatives, Steve Norris was always going to be hard to beat when he threw his hat into the ring again for the party's nomination. As in 2000, a string of others put their names forward, but when it came to a ballot of party members, he trounced his nearest rival, Roger Evans, the Assembly member for Havering & Redbridge, by more than three to one. He did attract a lot of criticism, however, for taking on the chairmanship in November 2003 of Jarvis, the engineering company which admitted legal liability for the previous year's rail accident at Potters Bar, in which seven passengers were killed.

The Liberal Democrat candidate in 2004 was Simon Hughes, the MP for Southwark & Bermondsey since a 1983 by-election. As the party's senior London MP, he had been widely expected to run in 2000, but after Paddy Ashdown's resignation had found himself running instead (unsuccessfully as it turned out) for the Liberal Democrat leadership.

Despite a slight increase in turnout from 2000 to 36.9 per cent, the conclusion once the votes were counted seemed to be that little had changed. Ken was re-elected for his second term, albeit with a slightly reduced share of the vote. He got 35.7 per cent of the first preferences, compared with Norris's 28.2 per cent (a slight increase on 2000) and Hughes's 14.8 per cent (also up on Kramer's position in 2000). After the redistribution of second preferences, Ken had 55.4 per cent of the vote to Norris's 44.6 per cent.

Labour had less to be cheerful about in the Assembly election, where the Conservatives managed to retain nine seats but Labour won only seven (down two on 2000). The Liberal Democrats managed to gain an extra seat, taking their tally to five, whilst the Greens lost one of their existing seats to retain just two and the UK Independence Party – helped by the fact that the election was on the same day as the elections to the European Parliament – won two seats for the first time.

The changing face of London, 2000–2008

London changed massively during Ken Livingstone's eight years as Mayor. Some of the alterations are hard to see at first – like a cleaner river Thames and changes in policing. Others, such as the removal of London's iconic Routemaster buses and the introduction of a fleet of 'bendy buses', are much more visible. Some were the very direct result of mayoral decisions; over others, for example the phenomenal influx of foreigners to London's multicultural and multi-ethnic melting pot, he was powerless (even if happily so). But the political landscape in 2008 was much less favourable to Ken than it had been four years previously: everything he had done, his decisions good and bad, affected almost every voter, and in what would turn into a fantastically close race, every change could turn out to be important.

The change to London over which the Mayor had least control was immigration, which has been rising consistently since the mid-1990s. In the first five years after Ken became Mayor London's population grew by 200,000, to 7.5 million. Yet this figure conceals the extent of international migration – almost 200,000 people a year moved to London from overseas, whilst only about 100,000 went the other way. These figures aren't absolute – London is a gateway city and some international migrants later moved to other parts of the UK – but they do shed light on a trend which most Londoners have observed. And it changed many other facets of life in the capital. Increasing numbers of foreign doctors staffed its hospitals and foreign teachers its schools; foreign cleaners, domestic staff, plumbers, electricians and bar and restaurant staff maintained its homes and catered to its leisure needs. London became ever more of a magnet for foreign bankers and lawyers, who moved to the city and became among the highest earners in the country (even if they didn't always pay their taxes here). These migrants boosted the economy, used public transport, enriched London's cultural life, and put extra pressure on London's costliest and cheapest housing alike; they sometimes made it harder for badly trained Londoners to find jobs and apprenticeships; they forced the police to work in ever more languages; and they provided a new focus for the far right and challenges for politicians across the political spectrum. Most intriguingly, 180,000 of them were eligible to vote on 1 May 2008, a larger number than Ken's majority in 2004. And whilst they were highly unlikely to all vote for one candidate and swing the election so directly, there was a large pool of votes there, and all the candidates knew it.

Ken was very proud of his increasingly international city and made promoting equality and multiculturalism an important part of his mayoralty. Among other things he brought in the race equality campaigner Lee Jasper as his adviser on equalities and policing and promoted various festivals around the city, which quickly became a part of London's cultural life. Funding for organisations aimed at ethnic minority groups rose. Ken's success in supporting multiculturalism was one of his proudest boasts during the election campaign, and it seemed to be part of the appeal to members of the International Olympic Committee when on 6 July 2005 they awarded London the 2012 Games. London's strong sense of identity was on display, too, the following day – after four young men blew themselves up on London's Tubes and buses. The city's response to the events of what became known as 7/7 was not a retreat into racism and sectarianism but, led by its Mayor, a confident assertion of its multicultural identity. And whatever else his enemies said about Ken, they all praised him for his leadership and his response after those terrible events. 'This was not a terrorist attack against the mighty and the powerful,' he said with a look of grim determination on his face. 'It was not aimed at Presidents or Prime Ministers. It was aimed at ordinary, working-class Londoners, black and white, Muslim and Christian, Hindu and Jew, young and old. It was an indiscriminate attempt to slaughter, irrespective of any considerations for age, for class, for religion, or whatever. That isn't an ideology, it isn't even a perverted faith – it is just an indiscriminate attempt at mass murder and we know what the objective is. They seek to divide Londoners. They seek to turn Londoners against each other.

'I said yesterday to the International Olympic Committee that the city of London is the greatest in the world, because everybody lives side by side in harmony. Londoners will not be divided by this cowardly attack. They will stand together in solidarity alongside those who have been injured and those who have been bereaved, and that is why I'm proud to be the Mayor of that city.'

As a long-time supporter of gay rights, Ken introduced other measures to make the city more accommodating to diversity, too. On 5 September 2001 Ian Burford and Alexander Cannell became the first gay male couple and Linda Wilkinson and Carol Budd the first lesbian couple to formally register their partnerships with the city. This, the establishment of the first civil partnerships register, paved the way for the 2004 Civil Partnership Act. It was not a marriage, said Burford, 'but a recognition of the value of a partnership'. Strictly speaking Ken had no powers in this area but he found something he could do and it helped lead to a wider change.

In all these areas Ken sought to promote a sense of London as a city apart and of being a Londoner as an identity to which people from all backgrounds could feel some allegiance. He joked about having a border with Surrey where people would show their passport and change their money. In a sense this was 'London nationalism', and it was very much in keeping with London's history. For hundreds of years before the conquest of 1066 London was essentially a city state, generating most of the country's wealth and governing itself, separate from the rest of the country. Kings and would-be kings alike had to reconcile themselves to London's place apart if they hoped to harness its power. Whilst it wasn't quite like that in the twenty-first century, there was certainly a more powerful sense of identity in 2008 than there had been in 2000, even if many in the outer boroughs still felt more a part of Essex, Kent or Surrey than they did of London.

If that sense of identity and community cohesion had indeed helped to win the Olympic Games for London, it promised to add huge new responsibilities to the Mayor's already overflowing in-tray. The Games would require massive infrastructure work in some of the most deprived parts of east London, phenomenal management control to stop costs spiralling (as they had in many other host cities), and civic leadership to prepare the city for the Games. Ken had set out his legacy commitments – more job, business, volunteering and sporting opportunities; transforming east London; keeping the Games sustainable; showcasing London as a diverse, creative and welcoming city; and keeping Londoners' contribution to the cost, through council tax increases, down to 38p a week. During the campaign he would challenge each of the other candidates to explain how London would benefit with them at the helm.

He did so on another major issue of international scope, too. Ken's pitch in 2008 was heavily based around meeting long-term challenges and there could be none more far-reaching in terms of potential impact and cost of avoidance than climate change. With policies on greening London's transport infrastructure and promises to reduce energy waste in London's buildings, Ken put the issue on the agenda and he received warm praise from other civic leaders from around the world for his initiatives. But was London in 2008 really that much more prepared to meet the challenges than it had been eight years earlier, and was climate change an issue which excited many voters?

One issue which certainly did exercise them was crime. Policing in London had undergone several dramatic changes since 2000. First came Lord Macpherson's inquiry into the police investigation of Stephen Lawrence's death, which found the Metropolitan Police guilty of 'institutional racism' and demanded reform. In the short term this produced major changes to the conduct of 'stop and search', and in the longer term a transformation in the way the Met handled its relations with minority ethnic communities. Neighbourhood policing has been another major change to the way the city was policed, both pressed for by Ken and fitting closely with policy from successive Home Secretaries. And huge quantities of cash from the Home Office allowed an enormous recruitment drive to take place – London's police force went from 25,000 in 2000 to 31,000 eight years later, not including around 4,000 police community support officers. Perhaps most importantly, overall crime fell.* But it ebbed and flowed: not all crime fell all the way through the period. Unfortunately there was no ebbing in one particular category which would become a huge issue during the election campaign – shootings and stabbings among young people. This culminated in 2007 and

* By how much depends on the two different sets of figures. Police recorded crime is exactly that, and subject to underreporting and reporting errors; the British Crime Survey is generally regarded as more accurate, providing details of people's experience of crime, but excludes some important categories of crime. The candidates would use different figures at different times during the campaign to make their point.

early 2008 with a terrible spate of twenty-seven teenagers killed in 2007 and eleven more by the time of the mayoral election in 2008. As well as concerns about violence, a new catchphrase, 'anti-social behaviour', entered the public consciousness as the Labour Government nationally attempted to bear down on small crimes and nuisance behaviour which caused acute discomfort and distress, often in the poorest neighbourhoods. Both of these types of crime, and the best way to tackle them, were among the hottest topics during the mayoral campaign.

In this, as in several other areas, the Mayor was not without powers to effect change, but neither was he master of all he surveyed. He could set the police budget, through the Metropolitan Police Authority, and as part of the 2007 Greater London Authority Act gained the power to appoint the chair of the MPA (or chair it himself). He did not, though, have the power to hire or fire Sir Ian Blair, Commissioner of the Metropolitan Police and the country's most senior police officer, who remained accountable only to the Home Secretary. Blair became the subject of considerable political controversy after the police shot dead an innocent Brazilian electrician, Jean Charles de Menezes, on 22 July 2005, in the frantic search for suicide bombers whose bombs had failed to go off in London the day before. Blair was sharply criticised for continuing to make factually incorrect statements about the shooting for some time after de Menezes's death and long after other senior police officers had known them to be incorrect, and for trying to prevent the Independent Police Complaints Commission from investigating the shooting. He fell out particularly badly with one senior officer, Deputy Assistant Commissioner Brian Paddick, who found it hard to believe that Blair had been so out of the loop at such a critical time and eventually left the Met.

The capital's creaking transport system had been the biggest political issue in 2000 and still loomed large in 2008. It was the policy area over which the Mayor, through the Transport for London agency, had the greatest control and the area in which Ken had taken greatest advantage of his powers. His transport policies were some of his best known and most controversial.

Top of the list in 2000 was the Tube. Experts suggested that it needed about £13 billion of investment to bring it up to spec – modernising the rails, the signalling and the station infrastructure. But how that money would be raised was intensely controversial. The government favoured a public–private partnership (PPP), which would hand control of the infrastructure to private companies; those companies would raise the necessary capital themselves, do the work and bear the risk, all for a fixed price. It would leave London Underground, which would remain in the public sector, to operate the trains. For a government which was already planning to invest record sums into the public sector, this had the overwhelming advantage that the £13 billion would not appear on the Government books as public borrowing. But it caused a huge row between Ken and the then Chancellor of the Exchequer, Gordon Brown. The new Mayor and his new Transport Commissioner, the American Bob Kiley, went so far as to take the Government to court over it, arguing that private borrowing was much more expensive than either direct government borrowing or a bond issue raised against future ticket sales. What was more, they argued, since the Mayor was now in charge of the Tube, he should decide how the finance was raised. The Government won the legal battle, the PPP went ahead as planned and for several years the repair and upgrade work proceeded under the two consortia – Tube Lines and Metronet – which had been awarded the contracts, but the two groups would produce dramatically different results. Tube Lines was a consortium of project managers which put the various contracts out to tender at the best price. Metronet, by contrast, was a consortium of contractors. Rather than use competitive tendering to get the best job done at the best price, its 'tied supply chain' meant the consortium generally used its own members. The predictable end result was that in July 2007 Metronet, operating badly behind schedule and in massive debt, collapsed. Ken was in like a shot, with TfL the only bidder to take over the contract. In what was effectively a renationalisation the Government paid off Metronet's PPP debt and eventually transferred the whole company to TfL, which in turn announced that it would operate a competitive bidding process for the remaining elements of the contract.

Ken had been busy renationalising elsewhere on the train network, too. The North London line, run under franchise by Silverlink Trains, had long been a target. It was regarded as one of the worst in the capital – the London Assembly had called it 'shabby, unreliable, unsafe and overcrowded'. In November 2007 TfL finally took it over, Ken rebranding it 'London Overground', spending money on increased staffing, improved safety and station facilities, and introducing Oyster cards across the line. It would eventually be joined outside the Tube network but under the TfL umbrella by the East London line, which closed for major work at the end of 2007. The aim was to make it a major transport artery, linking London's suburbs.

The largest infrastructure project agreed during the past eight years only just got off the ground as the 2008 mayoral campaign was beginning. This was the long-standing Crossrail proposal, originally mooted as far back as 1974; it was dusted off again in the early 1990s before being shelved and resuscitated once more. Crossrail will be a new line running across London, from Maidenhead in the west, via Heathrow, through central London and the City, to Shenfield in the east. It will be a major development for the City in particular, providing a direct link with Heathrow for the first time, and will relieve congestion on the existing Tube network by increasing capacity by a full 10 per cent. Due for completion in 2017, its £16 billion cost will be met by TfL, the Government and the City.

The railways had not been the only mode of transport to face major upheaval over the last eight years. In fact since much of the investment on the railways was in track and signalling, it was on the roads where the most dramatic changes could actually be seen. Two central policies significantly changed road transport in London between 2000 and 2008: the congestion charge and the massive spending on buses.

Ironically Ken's highest-profile policy had affected a mode of transport of which, as a non-driver, he had relatively little experience: cars. In 2000 congestion was widely seen as one of the city's most intractable problems and Ken's manifesto that year promised to introduce a congestion charge. The Labour Government had given local authorities the power to do so and Ken pressed ahead. The scheme was initially based on a £5 daily charge to come into the centre of the city. CCTV cameras would identify cars by their registration numbers and drivers would have to pay on the day or face a fine of £80. Initially it had a dramatic impact: after its first full year of operation TfL announced that traffic had fallen by 15 per cent whilst congestion had fallen by 30 per cent.

Over time, though, the benefits seemed to diminish and by 2007, even though traffic in the zone had fallen further still, congestion was back up almost to the pre-congestion charge level. And that was despite a raised charge and extended zone, to £8 from July 2005 and into Kensington and Chelsea from February 2007. The latter scheme proved particularly controversial among residents of the new zone, who would now have to pay 10 per cent of the daily charge to drive their cars or just keep them parked on the street.*

---

* Although there was no charge if the car was parked in a residents' parking bay.

Other critics pointed out that these new residents would now have no incentive not to drive into the original zone when they previously might not have done: TfL's own study suggested the western extension would cause an increase in traffic in the existing zone of some 2 per cent. No-one was able to answer the question of what would have happened to congestion had the charging zone not been introduced in the first place.

TfL also came under attack for resequencing large numbers of traffic lights in central London in such a way that they exacerbated the congestion problems. Boris Johnson would point to one set of lights in Trafalgar Square which was green for just 12 seconds and red for 105 seconds. Ken argued that traffic lights had been resequenced to provide extra time for pedestrians to cross the road. He, and TfL, also blamed the utility companies for many of the delays, particularly Thames Water, which was replacing large sections of the city's Victorian water mains.

Still, if cars were coming off the roads, travellers would need an alternative, and with an increasingly congested transport system and little prospect of much extra capacity being generated on the Tube for the foreseeable future, the bus network was a key part of TfL's plans. Ken directed heavy investment into buses, both financially and politically, as he sought to move people out of their cars onto the Tube in outer London, and free up space on the Tube by moving them to the buses in central London.

The investment was massive. In 2000 the bus network required no subsidy but by 2008 it was being subsidised to the tune of more than £600 million a year. Some of this came from congestion charge receipts, which by law had to be spent on public transport, and much came from the general TfL pot. It was spent on every aspect of the service – lowering fares (initially at least), new buses, more frequent services, new routes – all designed to make using the buses both more appealing and more practical. Much more controversially, Ken oversaw the gradual removal of the iconic Routemaster bus from London's streets – even though he had promised to save it, claiming in 2001 that 'only some ghastly, dehumanised moron would want to get rid of the Routemaster' (a quote which Boris would endlessly throw back at him during the campaign). Today Routemasters remain on only a small number of 'heritage' routes. They were partially replaced by a fleet of fuel-efficient and disabled-friendly 'bendy buses', which soon faced three problems. Firstly, they took up much more road space than the buses they replaced, and even if they could carry more people they caused endless blockages and seemed dangerous for cyclists. Secondly, because they had doors opening all along but no conductors, they seemed to offer an open invitation to fare evaders and soon became known as 'free buses'. And thirdly, well, they weren't Routemasters: no-one was ever going to love them. All three issues would remain controversial and would be the subject of heated discussion during the election campaign.

Many opposition politicians questioned whether Londoners got good value for all the extra money spent on buses, but in 2005 even the London Assembly's transport committee, chaired by a Conservative, concluded that they did. And looking at the figures it is hard to argue that the improvements were not dramatic: London's bus fleet grew to 8,000 vehicles and more than 700 routes, with a doubling of night routes. And bus ridership exploded, with an extra 600 million passenger journeys per year.

One further transport innovation hit London during those eight years: the introduction of the Oyster card. For those developing transport policy in the 1990s the buzzword was 'integration'. When Labour finally gained power after eighteen years in opposition John Prescott put integration at the heart of his transport policy and every Transport Minister since has paid obeisance to the idea. Yet Ken is the only Labour politician to have delivered substantial integration. By allowing people to put money onto an electronic card and thereby ridding much of the network of dealing with large quantities of cash, Oyster cards have sped up transactions (particularly on the buses) and made it much easier to switch between different modes of transport. The remaining challenge, to be tackled by whoever was elected Mayor in 2008, was how to fully 'Oysterise' National Rail services into London.

If most of the money spent in London went underground, Ken's new buses were not the only change which was visible above ground. In fact some of the most obvious changes were in London's public places and built environment.

The first place to be transformed had been one of London's grimmest public spaces: Trafalgar Square. This potentially wonderful space, home to the National Gallery, Nelson's Column, South Africa House and thousands of pigeons, had previously contrived to appear much less than the sum of its parts. It was effectively a giant round-about, dirty and dangerous, and the transformation has been remarkable. Traffic was rerouted so that there is a single pedestrian area from the gallery on the north side all the way to the column and the fountains, and new steps and paving were laid. It is now a logical place to meet, a gathering point, and it is used for regular concerts and cultural events – everything from the Russian Winter Festival to the St George's Day food festival and Mayor's Disability Rights Festival. The only change which still causes debate is the fate of the pigeons – they used to be fed by tourists who bought their pigeon feed from a small stall in the square. No more: much to the fury of the rapidly established Pigeon Alliance campaign the stall was closed, and a hawk was brought in to make sure they don't make a full-scale return.

More significant for the long-term future of London's vistas and horizon has been the use Ken made of his powers to set planning and development strategy. His eight years at the helm coincided with a massive building boom, and he was an enthusiastic promoter of tall buildings and those who built them, what he jokingly called the 'Militant Developer Tendency'. Some, such as the Swiss Re tower (widely known as the 'Gherkin') have already risen to take their place on London's skyline; others, such as the 'Shard of Glass' at London Bridge, are under construction; still others have yet to leave their architects' drawing boards. Guidance in the 2004 London Plan was that these very tall buildings should be approved if they would create 'attractive landmarks enhancing London's character, help to provide a coherent location for economic clusters of related activities or act as a catalyst for regeneration'. Ken has estimated that there will be fifteen more built over the next twenty years.

Under the 2007 GLA Act the Mayor's role over planning in the capital was strengthened, but he also received new powers over, and a substantial budget for, housing. These powers include: transferring the responsibilities of the London Housing Board to the Mayor; requiring him to prepare and publish a statutory London housing strategy and a strategic investment plan, setting out the priorities to meet the housing needs of all Londoners; and deciding the broad distribution of the affordable-housing part of the Regional Housing Pot in line with the strategy. In short, the Mayor will decide how £4 billion of public money for new affordable housing will be spent between 2008 and 2011. The same Act handed the Mayor substantial new powers and a budget for adult skills; additional strategic powers in areas including waste, culture and sport, health and climate change; and the right to make more appointments, in particular either to appoint the chair of the Metropolitan Police Authority or to chair it himself. It formed part of a wider second phase of devolution to the Welsh and Northern Ireland Assemblies, in which Ken had argued strongly for greater responsibility and autonomy for the Mayor of London.

In housing policy, Ken shored up his case for greater powers by pointing to his record in delivering affordable housing at a time when it became increasingly necessary. Between 2000 and 2008 house prices in London more than doubled, vastly outstripping pay increases.* It meant parts of the city were effectively off limits to anyone on a low or even middle income, and affordability became a major issue, including for many in the poorer-paid public services. Ken introduced a target that 50 per cent of new home developments should be affordable, but critics complained that he often approved and even promoted developments which failed to meet that target. In response Ken argued that many of the developments which fell under 50 per cent provided other social benefits, for example transport or other community facilities, or they were built on contaminated land which needed to be cleaned up first. He also complained that not all London boroughs were keen to support his 50 per cent target (this was not the only area of friction between the Mayor, charged with taking a strategic view of London's problems, and the boroughs, with inevitably more local concerns). Critics would also point out that much 'affordable housing' was not actually very affordable, with some going on the market for several hundred thousand pounds. But house-building did increase during the period, and by the time of the 2008 election Ken was promising 50,000 affordable houses over the next few years. All of these claims and counter-claims – and the candidates' proposed solutions to the problems of affordable housing in London – would be debated at length during the 2008 campaign.

Another issue would be the state of the economy, which had

* From an average of £144,852 to £304,781, according to Halifax figures.

boomed almost continuously between 2000 and 2008 and, unhelp-fully for the incumbent Mayor and Prime Minister, started spluttering just as major elections loomed. The economy had boomed particu-larly strongly in London: in a UK economy which had itself grown substantially, London's share grew from 16.3 per cent in 2000 to 17 per cent by 2005. But this growth was far from evenly spread. There was, in the words of the London Plan, a 'massive substitution of jobs in business services for jobs lost in manufacturing'. Grinding poverty remains alongside extraordinary success and wealth – the gleaming glass towers of Docklands still sit next to the benighted tower blocks of Tower Hamlets. The average weekly income of house-holds in London, at £766, is almost 30 per cent higher than the national average, but this too masks enormous variation. A quarter of households receive more than £1,000 per week whilst for 14 per cent the figure is less than £150. And although London boasts some of Britain's highest-paid workers, its employment rate has remained stubbornly below that for the rest of the country and has fallen slightly since 2002, whilst the unemployment rate in London has risen. As Mayor, Ken was a great advocate of the City and its potential for generating wealth and attracting talent. He understood that retaining the City's pre-eminence in financial markets was central to maintaining London's cutting edge (and the threat to it when the job losses started midway through April 2008). But he was also responsible for economic development and regeneration through the London Development Agency and its £400 million annual budget. The use to which he put that money would be more closely examined than any of his other policies during the course of the campaign.

Had London stepped up its game between 2000 and 2008? Ken certainly argued so. On the campaign trail he would claim with monotonous regularity that in 2000 London was competing with cities such as Frankfurt; by 2008 it was rivalling New York for the title of greatest city in the world (although he never quite specified in what sense). What was unarguable is that the job of London Mayor was now on the map. The original responsibilities – setting strategies and budgets for development, policing, transport, planning and several other areas, and his general power to promote economic and social development, and environmental improvement, in London – had been supplemented not only by the 2007 GLA Act but by Ken's own expansion of what people believed the job entailed. Many of Londoners' top concerns really did fall outside the Mayor's remit – he and his successors would be powerless over the closure or 'service reconfigurations' of schools, hospitals and post offices. But after the Presidents of Russia, France and Portugal the Mayor has the largest individual mandate in Europe, and with control over a budget of more than £11 billion he is the single most powerful man in London. The election just about to get under way mattered to London, and it mattered to the candidates, too.

Ken Livingstone

Ken Livingstone has been a major figure in London politics for almost thirty years. As the last leader of the Greater London Council (GLC) he was there for the death of strategic government in London; as the first directly elected Mayor of the city he was there at its rebirth. Over the same period he has gone from bogeyman of the left – 'the most odious man in Britain' according to the *Sun* – to cuddly Ken, maverick and media personality, and (almost) back again. Many people have pointed to his flexibility as the key to his success, but he has been consistent on two things: he is a lifelong Londoner and a lifelong socialist.

His unique place in London's life was confirmed when in 2000 he defeated Tony Blair and the might of the New Labour spin machine to become London's first elected Mayor. And in the eight years after that he proceeded to impose himself on the city in a way which had been foreshadowed in the White Paper setting out what the Government hoped the mayoralty would achieve. The Mayor would have, it said, 'exceptional influence going well beyond the specific statutory and financial power of the office'. In 2008, at the height of its campaign to rid the city of Ken, the editor of the *Evening Standard* acknowledged that he had done exactly that and praised him for making the job of Mayor of London one worth having and one worth doing.

Kenneth Robert Livingstone was born in Streatham on 17 June

1945. He grew up in Streatham, Tulse Hill and West Norwood, and went to Tulse Hill Comprehensive School. The school impacted on the rest of his life in two important ways. Firstly, it kindled his love of natural history: he bought frogs, salamanders and newts. His fondness for these cold-blooded creatures would later be one of his most humanising traits when he was otherwise GLC bogeyman (Boris would call him 'King Newt'). The second impact of his Tulse Hill education was an interest in politics. His parents were both members of the Conservative Party but he took to left-wing politics early. And he was confirmed in his left-wing orientation when he got his first job, as a lab technician at the Chester Beatty cancer research unit in Fulham Road. He worked there on animal experiments, and during the 2008 campaign this work would briefly become an issue. More significant was his political development, though. He was suddenly surrounded by men from committed socialist backgrounds, and this was reinforced by a trip he took across Africa in 1966/67. He joined Labour in February 1969, just as many on the hard left were leaving for a more revolutionary brand of politics. It allowed him to rise through the ranks very fast – he was elected to Lambeth Council just two years after he joined the party. It also meant that his commitment to the left was a practical one, not one based on an intimate relationship with the philosophy of Trotsky and the works of Marx, as it was for many his leftist comrades.

Two years after his election to Lambeth Council, having spent that time as vice-chair of the housing committee, he was elected to the GLC. Initially representing Norwood, his existence for the next thirteen years would be a peripatetic one as he shifted between three different GLC seats. Ken would serve on the council until its abolition in 1986, and it was also a period in which he came to public prominence and finessed his political modus operandi.

It is easy to forget today just how much power the hard left wielded in the Labour Party of the 1970s and early 1980s. This was particularly true after 1979 as the party, defeated by Margaret Thatcher's Conservatives in that year's general election, spiralled into destructive civil war. But for many on the left that war had been under way well before 1979, and on the GLC Ken was at the heart of it. Both his biographers paint a picture of a man plotting obsessively with various hard-left factions to promote their interests and their candidates on the GLC. Ken saw his opportunity in 1977. He had already moved to a safer seat when the Conservatives swept to victory in that year's GLC elections, defeating a slew of Labour members. He was one of the few left-wing members remaining and over the next four years he worked closely with the various leftist groups to get left-wing candidates selected to fight the seats at the next GLC elections, in 1981. His plotting paid off: those elections came at the height of the Thatcher Government's unpopularity and Labour in their turn swept to victory on the GLC. But if voters thought they were going to get the moderate Andrew McIntosh, who had defeated Ken to become Labour group leader the previous year, in charge of their council, they were very much mistaken. Within twenty-four hours of the election victory Ken, who had helped many of the new left-wing GLC members win their nomination battles, was the new Labour and council leader.

It was not long before he let London's voters know it. Within weeks he had rejected an invitation to the Prince of Wales's wedding to Lady Diana Spencer later that summer. He embraced positions on Northern Ireland and Israel which at the time were highly controversial, and over the next five years he would channel millions of pounds in subsidies to unpopular causes such as gay and lesbian activists, black rights groups and anti-war protesters. These positions made him deeply unpopular among some traditional Labour supporters, who weren't particularly enamoured of many of the causes. But for Ken it was what politics was all about. 'I think politics is not just looking at what is the most popular position to take and then taking it,' he said in 1983. 'Granted, some people come into politics because they want to line their pockets, others because they want a nice comfortable job. I came into politics because I wish to change society. And that means changing the hearts and minds of people. You start from an unpopular position and you plug away consistently. If you're right, eventually you win. I've no doubt at all that by the end of this century, if we continue to fight for it, we will be living in a Britain where there will be complete tolerance towards sexual preference … If the leadership of the party, as one of their standard positions, argue for women's rights, gay rights and a proper equal opportunities policy for blacks, we'll eventually change attitudes nationally.'

Most of these positions would later become part of the political mainstream, but in the early 1980s they were radical, almost revolutionary, and Ken worked closely with his hard-left factions to make progress on them. Many, most notably his outspoken support for Irish Republicanism, were well outside his area of responsibility, and they quickly made him enemies on Fleet Street. For him, the most significant was the *Evening Standard*. Its editorial on 24 July 1981 read: 'People, they say, get the politicians they deserve. Yet surely no-one – but no-one – deserves Mr Ken Livingstone. His rule at the Greater London Council goes straight into the cruel-and-unnatural-punishment class.' The sentiment was mutual. In 1983 Ken would withdraw all GLC advertising from the paper because of an allegedly anti-Irish cartoon it carried, worth up to £2 million over the next two years. This enmity was to wax and wane over the years – Ken would at one point write a regular column for the paper and he met his current partner, Emma Beal, there – but midway through his first mayoral term it would flare up again and the consequences would be far-reaching.

On the GLC his policies in areas that he did control were often almost as contentious as those which he didn't. Top of this list was

Tube and bus fares, and today his 'Fares Fair' policy is one of the few substantive policy achievements which anyone can remember from that time. It involved cutting fares, to be paid for by a supplementary rate.* In policy terms it was a success, with a dramatic increase in people – particularly commuters – travelling on the Tube, which at that time had a good deal of spare capacity. But levying a supplementary rate prompted one Conservative-run borough, Bromley, which contained no Tube stations, to challenge the policy in the courts. Bromley won in December 1981 and suddenly, not only was there no money to pay for the subsidy, but Ken had to put the fares up substantially above what they had originally been in order to pay the £125 million cost of the policy to date. It was a painful lesson, but it was well learned and twenty years later Ken would ensure that the legal grounds for the London congestion charge were much more carefully prepared.

That was not the end of Ken's assault on the ratepayers, though, and over the remaining few years of the GLC's life rates were to rise relentlessly. In fact by assuming in its budget that it would receive no Government funding, the GLC effectively thwarted the Conservative Government's attempts to control it. It escaped some of the popular fury which might otherwise have accompanied this ratcheting because it didn't issue its own rate bills – its rises were instead passed on as a 'precept' to the London boroughs. Amazingly the bills rose so high, and there was so little infrastructure in County Hall to process all the cash, that the GLC found it could not spend money fast enough.† For his pains its leader was to acquire the nickname 'Red Ken'.

---

* At the time local authority taxes, the rates, were paid by homeowners and were based on the value of the dwelling.

† County Hall was the GLC headquarters. Nowadays it is home to the Marriott County Hall hotel, the London Aquarium and, during the 2008 campaign, Boris Johnson's mayoral campaign HQ.

But the pains were not borne by Ken alone: ratepayers, national newspaper editors and Conservative MPs and ministers got increasingly frustrated with what they regarded as eccentric and dangerous leftism and the ostentatious rate increases. The Conservatives were particularly infuriated by Ken's decision to hang massive banners with London's unemployment figures on the roof of County Hall, almost directly opposite the House of Commons. Eventually Margaret Thatcher acted, including a pledge to abolish the GLC in her party's manifesto for the 1983 general election. During the next couple of years Ken would go to war with the Government over getting its manifesto commitment written into law. He would ultimately lose and the GLC was abolished on 31 March 1986, but Ken was a victor as well as a victim. Firstly, the campaign rehabilitated him personally; in many ways it was the making of him. Almost as important in the long run were the tactics – spending £50 million on advertising and publicity, branding everything from bins to traffic lights with the GLC logo. To his opponents this was political advertising and the taxpayer should not have footed the bill; to Ken any attempt to draw a distinction between political and non-political advertising was bogus. 'If you're trying to survive as we are in a hostile media environment ... you've got to have some way of explaining to the people who vote for you what you are doing and why,' he said. The *Londoner* newspaper and the ubiquitous branding would both be resuscitated when he became Mayor.

By the time the GLC was abolished Ken had found a safe berth elsewhere. He and his left-wing allies had waged a vicious, years-long and ultimately successful fight to deselect Reg Freeson, the moderate Labour MP for Brent East, and in the 1987 general election Ken was elected to Parliament.

Ken has always wanted to wield power. For him the struggles on the left were of interest only in so far as they furthered his objective of putting socialist policies into practice. And he wanted to be Prime

Minister. Yet in Parliament he was never able to reconcile his desire to speak out and be the 'People's Ken' with the need to comply and be a team player if he were to rise up the greasy pole. In addition to this the Labour Party of 1987, after four years of a strong rightward tide during Neil Kinnock's reforms, was very different to what it had been before. Ken and others on the left were soon stranded, and over the next ten years he increasingly became a politically irrelevant back-bench MP. Instead he carved out a career as 'cuddly Ken', spending time hob-nobbing with pop stars and celebrities, writing his auto-biography and columns in the *Evening Standard* and the *Sun*, appearing on *Have I Got News for You* and even popping up in cheese advertise-ments opposite the former Conservative Prime Minister Sir Edward Heath.

Yet he was not politically inactive. He remained strongly com-mitted to one leftist group, Socialist Action, and he spent thousands of pounds earned from his extracurricular activities on a hugely expensive computer system for economic modelling. When he finally returned to office as Mayor in 2000, the lessons learned and contacts made, both at the GLC and whilst in Parliament, were put to good use. Comrades from Socialist Action and others he had known for years, but unrelated to the group, were brought in to the highest levels of his new administration and would play a key part in the govern-ance of London over the next eight years. Among these were Simon Fletcher, his chief of staff, who was sometimes dubbed the 'deputy mayor'; John Ross, his director of economic and business policy; Redmond O'Neill, his director of transport and public affairs; Neale Coleman, his director of housing and regeneration; and Lee Jasper, his director of equalities and policing. The ex-Labour spin doctor Joy Johnson came in to perform the same task in City Hall. They would form the core of his kitchen cabinet, effectively running London for the eight years of his mayoralty, first outside the Labour Party and then back within it. In 2004 and again in 2008 a number of them would take time out from their formal duties to run Ken's re-election campaigns. They were joined by several people from outside Ken's inner circle, including Victoria Collins as the campaign press manager, Matthew McGregor from the Labour Party looking after digital communications, and Tessa Jowell, the Minister for the Olympics and London, and an important link between Ken and the Government.

Ken returned to the Labour fold just in time for the 2004 mayoral election. Tony Blair knew that forcing him to run as an independent again would be disastrous for Labour, and with Nicky Gavron, the existing candidate, willing to stand down, Ken was readmitted and became the Labour candidate. He had previously applied for readmission in 2002, but it was thought too early by many in the party and at that time the success of his highest-profile policy, the congestion charge, was by no means assured. Many, including some in the Government, gleefully predicted his fall from grace when it was introduced. For all his hostility to New Labour, Ken as Mayor worked successfully with Blair and many other ministers, and he gradually earned their respect for his policy successes and undoubted expertise about London. Not all his relationships were restored. A deep personal animus remained with Trevor Phillips which would occasionally boil over into public spats, for example, but it was a measure of Ken's reabsorption into the Labour fold that he was selected as the party's candidate for 2008 almost a year early and with barely a murmur of dissent.

There were certainly murmurs of dissent from other quarters. Most notably these came from the offices of the *Evening Standard*, two of whose staff had had run-ins with the Mayor in the past eight years. Both resulted in formal complaints about and investigations into Ken's behaviour. The first came in 2002 when the story emerged of a row at a party between Ken and his pregnant partner, Emma Beal, and a scuffle at the same party between Ken and a friend of

Beal's. The friend fell off a wall and was taken to hospital. Few parts of the story are uncontested, but the Liberal Democrats on the London Assembly eventually referred Ken to the Standards Board for England, a new quango with the power to investigate allegations of misconduct against politicians in local government. It subsequently cleared him. The next run-in, in February 2005 between Ken and a young *Standard* reporter, Oliver Finegold, was more serious. Finegold was speaking to guests as they left a reception at City Hall and as soon as he introduced himself as a reporter for the *Standard* Ken was on the offensive. 'Oh, how awful for you.' 'Have you thought of having treatment?' 'What did you do before? Were you a German war criminal?' he said as Finegold tried to ask about the Mayor's evening. So far, so rude, but when Finegold said he was Jewish and was quite offended at what the Mayor had just said to him, and asked again about his evening, Ken persisted: 'Well, you might be, but actually you are just like a concentration camp guard. You're just doing it 'cause you're paid to, aren't you?' The *Standard* itself didn't print the story; instead it somehow leaked to the *Guardian* and from there the row quickly escalated. Ken was in no mood to back down, attacking the *Standard* and Associated Newspapers, which owned it, and resolutely refusing to apologise, including for the offence he had caused to many Jews. The Board of Deputies of British Jews made a formal complaint and the Standards Board of England, which had considered the previous case, began a second investigation into Ken's behaviour. They referred the complaint to the Adjudication Panel for England, which in February 2006 ruled that Ken had failed to appreciate that his conduct was unacceptable. The panel, composed of three unelected adjudicators, proposed to suspend for four weeks the Mayor of London, elected with almost a million votes. The severity of the ruling undermined its legitimacy, and Ken later said that by overreaching themselves they had guaranteed that he would win. He eventually won his appeal against the panel, the judge ruling that whilst Ken had been 'unnecessarily offensive' he had the right to be so. Both affairs would have been much simpler if he had simply apologised, but, as he had shown throughout his career, Ken was not really the apologising kind. By the time of the 2008 election, the relationship between Ken and the *Evening Standard* was seen by some advisers as close to 'full-out war'.

If Ken had offended many Jews, he had a much stronger rapport with the Muslim community. It stretched back to the 1980s, when he was a strong supporter of Palestinian rights and a vociferous critic of Israeli policy in the occupied territories. After the 9/11 attacks he was a strident anti-war voice and courted the British Muslim community carefully, although some of his means were controversial. In 2004 he welcomed to City Hall Yusuf al-Qaradawi, an anti-Semitic, homophobic and sexist preacher who is regarded as the spiritual head of the Islamist Muslim Brotherhood. Al-Qaradawi openly supports suicide bombings against Israel but had criticised the 9/11 attacks. Following a pattern he had set when controversially engaging with Sinn Fein during the 1980s, Ken argued that the West needed to engage with figures such as al-Qaradawi who had credibility when they criticised al-Qaeda. Some observers noted that his embrace of al-Qaradawi had the added benefit of appealing to many Muslim voters.

Much of Ken's record as Mayor is covered in the previous chapter but it is worth mentioning here his foreign excursions. London had no formal foreign policy, but in two distinct ways he used his office to assert the city's position on the international stage. First were the outreach efforts: expensive trips to India and China and the establishment of so-called 'Kenbassies', London offices in Beijing, Brussels, Caracas, Delhi and Mumbai. Ken argued that all these generated far more by way of investment in London than they cost. Second was his courting of two Latin American potentates, Fidel

Castro in Cuba and Hugo Chávez in Venezuela. Both had very questionable human rights records, yet Ken set about praising the former and doing a substantial oil-for-advice deal with the latter. The deal with Chávez would provide Ken with approximately $24 million a year, allowing him to offer half-price bus travel for poor Londoners; in return Venezuela would receive advice from Transport for London on how to run a public transport system. The Venezuelans seemed more interested in the propaganda value of the deal and, according to Andrew Hosken, one of Ken's biographers, several of Ken's inner circle also regarded it primarily as an ideological victory. Boris Johnson was not the only one who considered this dabbling in foreign policy 'crackers'.

Boris Johnson

Alexander Boris de Pfeffel Johnson is almost unique in political life in that he is known and nearly universally referred to by the public by that single name, 'Boris'. Whilst some of his initial journalistic efforts were credited to 'Alexander Johnson' and his family still call him Al, the Boris branding has been used for virtually his whole professional life.

Towards the end of the 2008 mayoral campaign, Tessa Jowell, the Minister for London, was reported as saying that any Cabinet ministers caught referring to him in such informal terms would be liable to a £5 fine, since she deemed it to be encouraging voters to view him with affection. But it is interesting to note that one of the very few other politicians who has so often been called merely by his first name is 'Ken' himself.

And the similarities with Ken do not end there. In the introduction to his biography, *Boris: The Rise of Boris Johnson*, Andrew Gimson stated: 'He reaches far beyond the ranks of those who are interested in politics, and attracts support even among those who hate politicians,' a description which could also be assigned to Ken. Likewise, the following description of the 1980s-mould Ken – from Mark d'Arcy and Rory MacLean's account of the 2000 mayoral election, *Nightmare! The Race to Become London's Mayor* – could equally be ascribed to Boris in his ascendancy: 'His political notoriety made Livingstone a star. Television couldn't get enough of him; he was a

natural media performer, candid, articulate, reasonable, funny ...
[his] self-deprecating flippancy proved irresistible on screen.' Yet
whilst they have both revelled in being overly candid political maver-
icks with a lot of media savvy, they are poles apart in terms of their
political and social backgrounds.

So what were Boris Johnson's origins? A brief mention should be
made here of his Turkish ancestry. When plagued by accusations of
Islamophobia or racism during the campaign, he pointed to his
Muslim forebears, most notably his great-grandfather Ali Kemal Bey,
a Turkish journalist, novelist and politician who Boris claimed could
recite the Koran by heart. And despite talking often during the mayoral campaign about growing up in London, Boris's childhood was
actually somewhat nomadic.

Born in New York in 1964, he came to England with his mother
not long after his birth so that she could finish her studies at Oxford,
but the city where he would later shine as a student did not remain
home for long. There followed stints of varying lengths at the
Johnson family farm on Exmoor, in Washington and New York again
and in London, where he resided variously in St John's Wood, Maida
Vale and several addresses in Primrose Hill.

He spent several years at primary school in that vicinity before
being moved to Brussels at the age of nine, because his father got a
job at the European Commission, but two years later he was
despatched to board at Ashdown House, a prep school in East Sussex.
From there he went to Eton College as a King's Scholar. He flour-
ished at Eton, although school reports cited in Gimson's biography
reveal a lack of effort and preparation in both academic work and
debating, but his performances on the stage are praised and in fact he
was eventually made captain of the college.

By the age of fourteen Boris's parents had divorced and he was
living with his mother in another district of the city which he would

one day run: Notting Hill, spiritual home to David Cameron's new-look Conservatives three decades in the future. Not only was the future Conservative leader, of course, a fellow pupil two years below Boris at Eton, but they both went up to Oxford, and the two future Oxfordshire MPs both appear in the notorious 1987 photo-graph of members of the riotous Bullingdon Club, unearthed by Francis Elliott and James Hanning for their biography, *Cameron: The Rise of the New Conservative*.

Boris won a scholarship to Balliol College, Oxford, where he is said to have wanted to achieve three goals: become president of the Oxford Union, find a wife and take a first-class degree. He succeeded in the first two (although his first marriage would be shortlived and he would later marry Marina Wheeler).

The Oxford Union has launched the political careers of countless politicians and it would seem that Boris had early designs on joining them, according to several sources quoted by Gimson. One close friend is cited as reporting that 'at the age of eighteen he set himself the target that he was going to be in the Cabinet by the age of thirty-five'. Another contemporary reckoned that 'his secret ambition was to be President of the United States', which, since he had been born there, was not unattainable either. Boris's sister Rachel, meanwhile, recalls that her older brother's early childhood desire had been to be 'world king'.

The job of London Mayor did not exist at that time, so we can only speculate as to whether he would have considered it a suffi-ciently high-ranking role for which to aim. In any event, it was at the Oxford Union that he honed the skill he used to such great effect in later life of winning over an audience with his characteristic bum-bling, buffoonish style. It helped propel him to the presidency of the union, and Gimson concluded that the style was learned from his father:

> They talk in an amazingly similar way, and Boris has learned a great part of his comic art from his father. They behave like stage Englishmen, often pretending to be impossibly baffled and stupid, while behind this screen they calculate what would be to their own advantage. This manner makes it hard for them to do seriousness, nor do they detect any great public demand for it.

Another contemporary remembered him as 'the best showman of his generation'.

After Oxford, Boris spent the briefest of times as a management consultant before embarking upon a career in journalism, first at the *Times* and then at the *Daily Telegraph*, where he was taken on as a leader writer before a five-year stint as the paper's Brussels correspondent. After returning to work at the *Telegraph*'s London newsroom, he cut his teeth in serious politics as Conservative candidate in 1997 in a relatively safe Labour seat in north Wales. 'I fought Clwyd South but Clwyd South fought back,' as he remembers. But it boosted his profile; the first of seven appearances (yes, there have only been seven) on *Have I Got News for You* came in 1998 and the editorship of the *Spectator* was handed to him the following year.

However, he had not lost his thirst for politics and when the Conservative Association in the plum seat of Henley sought a replacement for Michael Heseltine in 2000, Boris put his hat in the ring and was chosen from the 202 hopefuls who had applied. There was no dilemma for him as to whether to dump journalism for politics: he opted to have his cake and eat it and continued in both fields. This often caused conflicts which would not finally be resolved until he left the *Spectator* in 2005.

It may have been due to those conflicts that his rise up the political ladder was not as fast as he might have wished. Made a

Conservative vice-chairman by Michael Howard in November 2003, he also became Shadow Arts Minister the following May. But in the autumn of 2004 several incidents – all with *Spectator* connections – would result in his sacking.

Firstly, there was the editorial in the magazine in which the city of Liverpool was charged with being 'hooked on grief' in the wake of the murder of a Liverpudlian hostage in Iraq, Ken Bigley. Howard forced Boris to visit the city to apologise in a day of high farce, and the humiliation he suffered for that alone was said to have put Boris on the brink of resignation. Then tabloid revelations emerged of an affair with his *Spectator* colleague Petronella Wyatt, who had aborted two children allegedly fathered by Boris. His denial (he memorably called the claims an 'inverted pyramid of piffle') and the subsequent realisation that he had lied about the situation prompted Howard unceremoniously to sack him. Yet he was not out of the limelight for long as his old friend David Cameron's elevation to the Conservative leadership in 2005 saw him swiftly rehabilitated as the party's higher education spokesman – although it was at that moment that the *Spectator* editorship had to be sacrificed.

By this stage in his career Boris had become something of a phenomenon, principally through his television appearances and his popularity as a guest speaker both at universities and at Conservative associations across the land. In retrospect, someone with such appeal to a broad cross-section of the public was an obvious choice to be candidate for London Mayor. But the Conservative Party went through a great deal of turmoil before it came to that conclusion.

It emerged in early April 2006 that the party was planning to hold a London-wide US-style primary that autumn to select its candidate for the 2008 mayoral election. The then party chairman, Francis Maude, launched the contest the following month, promising that 'every Londoner who supports the Conservative Party has the chance to be our candidate' and 'everyone on the electoral register in London will be able to have a say over who will be the Conservative candidate'. In the press release announcing the contest, Cameron added that 'headhunters will be used to encourage potential candidates to apply'. In other words, the search was on for a big name to don the Tory rosette.

There was immediate speculation over whether the previous candidate, Steve Norris, would put his name forward again (most reports suspected not), but the first 'big beast' said to be considering it was the former Metropolitan Police chief Lord Stevens. It was then reported that Sir Christopher Meyer, the former Ambassador to Washington, had been approached, but he rejected the suggestion outright.

Nick Ferrari, the populist host of the breakfast show on London radio station LBC 97.3, was another big name to be mooted, but his candidacy would face several difficulties. Firstly, becoming a candidate would probably have meant him having to give up his radio show, which not only paid the bills but gave him exposure to the public. Secondly, as a highly outspoken broadcaster, his views, although generally to the political right, would not necessarily chime with Cameron's modernising image. Ferrari had long taken the view that it would be a waste of public money for London to host the 2012 Olympics and in 2003 he had been rebuked for failing to cut off a caller who was delivering a xenophobic rant on the subject of asylum seekers (something for which Ken Livingstone attempted to get him sacked). Although he rejected the idea of standing for the Conservatives, Ferrari would later seriously consider running as an independent, although he would eventually write that his divorce 'effectively sidelined my ambitions'.

So the party's attempt to attract high-profile candidates was not going to plan. Other names who Conservative Campaign

Headquarters (CCHQ) had originally hoped might be persuaded apparently included TV presenters Anne Robinson and Andrew Neil, *Big Issue* founder John Bird and ex-army chief General Sir Mike Jackson.

There was a small flurry of applications from party activists in London, who would have applied in any case under the previous internal party selection system. Warwick Lightfoot and Victoria Borwick – both councillors in Kensington & Chelsea – along with the man who was runner-up to Norris in the rerun 2000 selection ballot, Andrew Boff, all put in early nominations, and they were eventually rewarded with places in the final run-off over a year later. Others to come forward were Assembly member Richard Barnes (whom Boris would appoint a Deputy Mayor), James Cleverly (who would be elected Assembly member for Bexley & Bromley at the election) and Eurosceptic activist Lee Rotherham, standing on an abolitionist ticket.

The one name to stand out from the crowd at that stage was that of Nick Boles, an openly gay former Westminster councillor and ex-parliamentary candidate for Hove, who was by then heading the distinctly 'Cameroon' think tank Policy Exchange. Close to many in the Cameron inner circle, he looked likely to put up the most serious challenge for the job.

But then on 4 August, eight weeks after nominations had opened, Maude suspended the whole process, clearly frustrated by the lack of big hitters expressing an interest. He claimed that there had been 'a number of excellent applications', but in a snub to the existing applicants, he added: 'We have also received expressions of interest from a number of very serious potential candidates for whom the timescale we originally set is too restrictive.' The deadline was therefore extended, but he nonetheless said that the process would continue 'with a view to selecting a candidate next spring'.

A trickle of further candidates continued to put themselves forward. Among the more quirky prospectuses was that of Penny Mordaunt, already the Conservatives' prospective parliamentary candidate for Portsmouth North, where she lives, but a daily commuter into London. Her complaint was that commuters were the lifeblood of the capital's economy, yet had no say over the city's leadership. In December 2006, it also emerged that Mike Read – the former Radio 1 DJ and one of the 'showbiz' names occasionally to be spotted at party fundraisers – had registered his interest in standing.

Boles's position as frontrunner was again confirmed in the New Year, when he announced that he was leaving his job to concentrate on securing the mayoral nomination, although there was renewed speculation at that time that Norris might yet join the race. Brian Paddick, the eventual Liberal Democrat candidate and former senior police officer, would also later claim to have been approached by the Conservatives around this time. John Bird also took the opportunity to announce that he would not be seeking the Conservative nomination, and that he would rather stand for the job as an independent candidate (although he didn't in the end). And news later came that former CBI chief Sir Digby Jones had been approached by the party about standing, although he turned them down, later to accept a peerage from Gordon Brown and serve as a Government minister.

Spring had arrived and it was evident that Maude's timetable was going to have to slip again, almost making the selection fiasco for the 2000 race look smooth and organised by comparison. Desperate times call for desperate measures, they say, and the next chapter in the selection story confounded most observers.

The party had approached Greg Dyke, the former BBC director general, who was forced to resign over the Hutton report, with a view to him standing in the party's interest. What was remarkable about this was the fact that Dyke was fundamentally not a Conservative. In his youth he had been a Labour candidate for the Greater London Council and before joining the BBC had donated money to Labour in advance of the 1997 general election. After the Iraq War he joined the Liberal Democrats, although he had admitted on the record that he had already been voting Lib Dem for years in his constituency of Twickenham as he voted tactically – in other words against the Conservatives. The Dyke plan would involve him standing as a joint Conservative/Liberal Democrat candidate and even got as far as being discussed by David Cameron and Sir Menzies Campbell, the Liberal Democrat leader, in a face-to-face meeting.

On 18 April Maude confirmed that such discussions had taken place, but that the idea had been rejected by the Liberal Democrats. He also said that 'over forty' people had applied to be Conservative candidate by that stage. The following day, the final timetable for the party's selection process was announced: nominations would remain open until 16 July, with a ballot on a final shortlist to take place during September, meaning that the candidate would be unveiled at the party's conference in Blackpool – a year later than originally intended.

More unknowns reared their heads above the parapet as Conservative hopefuls: Bromley councillor Simon Fawthrop, Harrow councillor Lurline Champagnie and ex-boxer Winston McKenzie. He would eventually stand at the election as an independent, but it was becoming increasingly clear that the search for a big name to oppose Ken Livingstone – who by then had been readopted as Labour candidate – was eluding the party. Norris even spoke out to conclude that 'there aren't any serious candidates' and was therefore still considering standing himself. And as if to compound the party's difficulties, less than two weeks before the close of nominations, Boles, deemed the most serious of the declared candidates, was forced to withdraw after being diagnosed with cancer. (After his recovery, he would become Conservative candidate for Grantham & Stamford, whose sitting MP, Quentin Davies, had defected to Labour.)

But then, just as it looked as though Norris would become the candidate almost by default, it emerged that Boris Johnson was entering the race. Nick Robinson, the BBC's political editor, broke the news on 4 July, although the story seemed so implausible at the time that he didn't even push BBC bulletin editors to give it pride of place that night. Robinson suggested that Cameron had been behind the calls to get the Henley MP to run, although in a statement swiftly issued by Conservative HQ, Boris said, 'I want to stress that this idea did not come from David Cameron or from anyone in his office.' He didn't commit to run there and then, citing the obvious obstacle that he still represented a constituency nearly 40 miles from the centre of London (although he had of course lived primarily in the capital, latterly in Islington, for some years). But very quickly a head of steam built up behind him and it became obvious that he was the only candidate to have come forward (of supposedly around fifty) capable of generating the air of excitement about the selection process for which the party had been so desperate.

If nothing else, this was demonstrated by the media scrum that greeted him when he rolled up outside City Hall to officially announce his candidacy. He wheeled his bicycle through a pack of reporters and photographers with considerable difficulty, only to get on it and cycle off when he wanted to escape them after he'd said his piece. The chaotic event – which he described himself as a riot – was to belie a lack of organisation which would concern the party's campaign chiefs for some time.

With one candidate clearly head and shoulders above the rest, there was some speculation that there might even be a coronation rather than a contest, since several runners had already pulled out to 'back Boris'. However, the process having already suffered so many delays and setbacks, the last thing the party could have realistically done was to cancel the primary, its grand exercise in giving its candidate a London-wide democratic mandate before the actual election. The list of applicants was quickly whittled down to Boris and the aforementioned Andrew Boff, Victoria Borwick and Warwick Lightfoot, who would have about two months to put their cases. The Boris camp soon had reason to be cheerful, with an early (and prescient) YouGov sample of London voters indicating that, if chosen, he would lead Ken by 46 per cent to 40 per cent.

The public were invited to register for the primary and hustings were organised for early September in advance of ballot papers being issued, although the result was to all intents and purposes a foregone conclusion. Boris triumphed with 79 per cent of the vote – 15,661 votes to be precise – followed by Borwick, Boff and Lightfoot all with single figure percentages.

The aim of holding an open primary had been to capture the imagination of the electorate at large and get ordinary Londoners participating in the ballot in their tens and hundreds of thousands. In that respect it had singularly failed, and although no figures were issued, the proportion of non-party members among the less than 20,000 people taking part must have been very low. But then turnout in elections where everyone is convinced what the result will be before a single vote is cast always tends to be low. They do come out to vote, however, when there is a genuinely closely fought contest – as Boris and his fellow candidates would discover in May 2008.

Brian Paddick

Brian Paddick was the Liberal Democrat candidate. Tall, fit, articulate, standing ramrod straight whilst delivering short, clipped answers (always within the allotted time), he was the only non-career politician in a race of non-politicians. He regarded himself as a straight bat: telling it like it is, just as he had throughout a sometimes politically difficult police career. Being gay and a former policeman further distinguished him from the other contenders, and yet somehow he failed to catch the public imagination. Selected by the party – like Boris Johnson – mainly because he was the face most readily identifiable to the public, it quickly became apparent that he would be another third-placed Liberal Democrat. His main impact on the mayoral race, like Susan Kramer and Simon Hughes before him, would be the division of his second preferences, but unlike his predecessors (whose second preferences had gone disproportionately to Ken Livingstone) they split almost equally between the two main candidates.

Yet he might have played a more significant role, and at various points during the election campaign he and his team thought he stood a chance of winning the mayoralty. The calculation was the same as it had been in 2000 and 2004: if only their candidate could get through to the final round, the redistributed votes of those who had dropped out would likely push him over the top. But, as in 2000 and 2004, whilst the second-preference votes might have made that a possibility, the party would always fall at the first hurdle – first preferences. The Liberal Democrats had looked in a good position in mid-2007, when Tory desperation was made plain by their offers of electoral pacts or joint candidatures. The offer to Greg Dyke caused Menzies Campbell considerable embarrassment after it became known that he was considering it. Paddick, too, considered the offer for a few hours before turning it down. An anguished phone conversation with his mother seems to have swung him away from the Conservatives: '"How can I stand for the Conservatives when I'm a card-carrying Liberal Democrat?" I asked my mother. [She replied:] "Churchill did it. He crossed the floor." She paused for a moment. "But his mother never forgave him for it." I would never have forgiven myself for it either.'

That conversation contains the calculation that almost all the young, modernising and usually centre-right Liberal Democrats now running the party have made at some point in recent years: join the party whose philosophy you share and take the hard road or join the Conservatives and at least have the prospect of power some time soon.

Paddick was of course aware of the difficulties posed by the electoral arithmetic, but thought there was a chance he could overcome it with a swift (or relatively swift) one-two. First knock Boris on the head early by presenting him as an ineffective, inexperienced buffoon – funny and entertaining, certainly, but not the sort of chap you'd want running London. Ken would eventually put this argument at its snappiest: 'If this was a competition for permanent chairman of *Have I Got News for You*, I wouldn't even stand.' The Lib Dem plan was that once Boris was hobbled, Paddick could present himself as a credible alternative to Ken. To begin with, at least, Paddick didn't launch a full-frontal assault on the Mayor or his record.

It would be a mistake not to see Paddick as a politician – you simply do not rise to the position of Deputy Assistant Commissioner of the Metropolitan Police without some political skills. Ken acknowledged as much when in 2007 he and Paddick discussed the just-ex-police officer's chances were he to run for Mayor. What Paddick did lack, though, was experience of running for office as a Liberal Democrat. If he had, he would have known that Liberal Democrat candidates must work hard to justify themselves: they must prove – both to voters and to journalists – not only that they are good, but that a vote for them isn't going to be wasted. Lib Dem activists from the humblest parish councillor to the longest-serving parliamentarian understand this but Paddick had to find out the hard way. This steep political learning curve produced a great deal of frustration and appeared to be the root cause of many later difficulties.

He may not have had much of a history in the party, but Paddick did have one big advantage over most Liberal Democrat candidates and certainly over the two who opposed him in the Liberal Democrat selection battle, Fiyaz Mughal and Chamali Fernando: people had heard of him. By contrast Mughal, a Haringey councillor who was active in both party and wider non-profit circles, had little public recognition; similarly Fernando was impressive but little known. At one point it looked as though Lembit Öpik, the MP for Montgomeryshire and partner of Cheeky Girl Gabriela Irimia, might stand, but he didn't, and against much less well-known competition, a former senior Met commander with a national profile was always a likely shoo-in. Paddick swept to victory, winning 73 per cent of the Liberal Democrat first-preference vote when the results were announced on 13 November 2007. Amid high hopes in the party Vince Cable, the acting party leader, introduced him as the serious candidate, dismissing Boris with a typically withering assessment: 'I don't sense that even the Conservatives take their candidate very seriously.' At the press conference Paddick promised the assembled journalists: 'I'm not going to be like any politician you've ever seen before, and that's why I'm going to win.'

Certainly his life up until then had been like no police officer's life that anyone had seen before. The stories which brought him a national profile had also brought notoriety – as 'Britain's most controversial police officer' – and whilst they played little part in his fate as candidate for London Mayor they certainly helped form the man who ran for office: his sometimes testy relationship with the media, his sometimes stiff personality and his permanent focus on crime as Londoners' number one issue. The first time Paddick pricked the public consciousness was with the revelation that he had been contributing regularly to an anarchist website, Urban 75, signing on just as 'Brian the Commander'. This in itself may not have caused a scandal, but the fact that the Metropolitan Police commander in Lambeth went on to acknowledge that he found anarchism 'appealing' did. Paddick's argument that he had been engaging with different strands of the community did not cut much ice among the Met's top brass, and it put him on the radar screen for the tabloids, which would be even keener to cover him in the future. It meant he was something of a known quantity when the other big stories about him, both much more serious, both relating to his conduct in public office and both touching on the thorny issue of cannabis, erupted. The first, initiating the Lambeth drugs experiment, remains a cause of some pride to Paddick, or 'Commander Crackpot' as he now became known to readers of the *Sun*. Shortly after arriving in the badly understaffed borough, he told his Met bosses that cautioning people rather than arresting them for possessing small quantities of cannabis for personal use would save vital police time and enable his officers to focus on bigger criminal fish. It proved hugely controversial, the tabloids leading the attack with headlines about the 'Shock police drugs U-turn'.

Paddick persisted, though, and he can recite figures to show that the policy saved hundreds of police hours and actually led to more drugs seizures. Perhaps as important, he argues that it was exactly the type of policy which senior policemen were supposed to try: they should, he wrote, be 'expected to challenge the existing paradigm, to look at the world differently and convince others that their view of the world was the right one – to literally think outside the perceptual box'.

If Paddick was happy with some minor tabloid notoriety for thinking outside the perceptual box, the second story was much less welcome, and far more damaging to his reputation for probity and decency. A former partner gave an interview to the *Mail on Sunday* which was little short of a character assassination. It painted him as lonely and friendless, a man who regularly had casual sex with strangers in public, had failed to inform his superiors that his new partner was on bail when their relationship began and, sensationally for a senior police officer, had smoked cannabis 'hundreds of times'. Cue more screaming headlines along the lines of 'Gay cop grilled on dope'. Paddick was suspended by the Met, but was eventually cleared of the drugs charges and sued the *Mail on Sunday*, settling out of court. Nonetheless, the episode put another black mark against a police record which until that point had been exemplary. Indeed, these two incidents aside, from his CV Paddick appeared very well suited to the task of running London. First of all, like Ken, he is a lifelong Londoner. Born in 1958 in Balham, he was raised in Mitcham and Tooting, and educated in Sutton. He joined the Met straight out of school and rose quickly through the ranks. By November 1980 he had been promoted to sergeant and was posted to Brixton, 'the most valuable education' of his police life, he would later say. He was there for the riots in 1981 and to attempt policing the community afterwards. He is proud of knowing the patch and the people, and extremely proud that when he was removed as Lambeth borough commander they came onto the streets to protest at his removal. One poster read: 'The Life of Brian: he's not a naughty boy, he's the Messiah!' The lessons he learned in Lambeth – about police racism, sexism and homophobia, and about policing by consent – informed the rest of his police career and, come his turn to run for London Mayor, informed the policies he put forward for reform of the Metropolitan Police. In his autobiography he reported that Met surveys of how safe people felt put Lambeth on a par with Bromley, which is in fact much safer: 'I think that people's fear of crime is not simply about the amount of crime happening around them, or even whether or not they themselves have been the victims of crime, but about lack of trust and confidence in their local police service and their local police chief.'

For a man who had spent his whole career as a policeman, it should be no surprise that the two other factors in his background which made him unusual as a politician also formed an important part of his time in the police. The first was a business degree – earned during a brief interlude when the Met was getting worried about leadership. The second was a far more powerful part of who Paddick was – he was openly gay. Paddick says he knew from the age of about ten that he was different from the other boys, but in a police force not known for its tolerance and with a family which he didn't feel would have accepted him for who he was, he tried to hide it. He even married, although the marriage eventually broke down.

The end of Paddick's police career was precipitated by the death of the innocent Brazilian electrician Jean Charles de Menezes at the hands of Metropolitan Police officers on 22 July 2005. In the febrile atmosphere following the London Tube and bus bombings two weeks earlier, many – including, apparently, the Met Commissioner, Sir Ian Blair – initially thought they had shot a suicide bomber. Yet it soon became clear that they had not, and that Blair may have known sooner than he had admitted – a serious charge and one which Paddick initially thought he could substantiate. He later withdrew it, telling the inquiry that he could only be sure Blair's senior advisers knew, and that he found it inexplicable that they had not told their boss. As reformist allies, Paddick and Blair had at one time been close but, unsurprisingly, relations between the two men broke down around this time and after a couple of years of non-jobs around the Met a disillusioned Paddick retired from the force in 2007. The falling out and the pressures of the mayoral campaign would eventually lead Paddick to call for his former friend's resignation.

If the campaign was to see the end of some relationships, Paddick soon developed new ones in the party and with the team he built around him. Key figures were Andrew Reeves, the campaign manager, his press secretary Emily Walch and his press secretary-cum-aide Carina Trimingham. As with Boris, Paddick's small, UK-based team was eventually supplemented by talent from outside the UK in the form of Rick Ridder, the campaign's American strategist, and Jerome Armstrong, his American web guru.

The other candidates

The 2008 election was marked not just by the presence on the ballot paper of Boris Johnson, Ken Livingstone and Brian Paddick, but by a number of other interesting candidates. These ranged from long-time political activists who had run many times before to electoral neophytes.

The most experienced was Lindsey German, representing the Left List (part of the former Respect party). She had run in 2004, representing Respect, but the party had split in 2007 and was now divided between the Bethnal Green & Bow MP, George Galloway, and his supporters, and the Left List, which was backed by the Socialist Workers Party. As always on the hard left, the separation had been rancorous: Galloway's supporters changed the locks on the party HQ, whilst the SWP faction kept control of the party's website. German herself had made a mark as convener of the Stop the War coalition, and in the 2004 mayoral election she took a creditable fifth place. Of the minor parties, only the Christian Peoples Alliance beat her. That, though, had been at the time of the Iraq War and nobody expected her to perform quite as well in the less frantic political climate of 2008.

The only other woman in the race was the much less experienced but more media-friendly Green, Siân Berry. Berry had first made her name leaving leaflets on 4x4 cars telling their owners they shouldn't be using them in cities. A former 'principal speaker' of the Greens – they had only recently voted to move away from having one male and one female leader – she had to juggle the Green position in London with maintaining a clear identity for the party. Since the last mayoral elections, the Green Assembly members had backed much of Ken Livingstone's programme, allowing him to get his budget passed and increasing their own influence over the Mayor. Berry did a deal with Ken, making it clear that she hoped her second-preference votes should go to Ken and vice versa, and in some ways she would struggle for the rest of the campaign to assert her own identity. Still, as the presumptive fourth-placed candidate she was at least invited to some of the more significant mayoral hustings, at which she performed well. Her youth and easy humour fitted well with the other leading candidates, and the fact that she would be little more than a footnote to the final result meant her extraordinary list of commitments and non-existent explanation of how they would be paid for was never seriously challenged. She was the fourth-placed candidate on the party's Assembly list, and hoped that with a good performance in those elections she might just join her colleagues on the Assembly.

In 2004 the Greens had suffered because the mayoral and Assembly elections were held on the same day as those for the European Parliament. The big winners on that occasion were the UK Independence Party, which won two seats on the Assembly (and twelve in the Parliament, coming in third place). That result promised to provide a strong platform for 2008, but within months the party had descended into civil war and the GLA members had left to establish the One London party. Its leader, Damian Hockney, initially planned to stand for Mayor in 2008 but, faced with what he assailed as a 'media blackout' of minor parties and 'being banned from every mayoral hustings', he withdrew just before nominations closed. In reality, critics pointed out, his withdrawal was probably just as much about the thousands of pounds that would have been spent for an inevitably losing campaign as it was about the lack of media coverage (the £10,000 deposit is lost if the candidate doesn't attain 5 per cent of first-choice votes – all the minor candidates would lose theirs). Hockney's candidacy would only ever have been about raising the profile of One London for the Assembly elections, and in that sense he was in the same boat as all the minor parties putting up a slate of candidates, including his old colleagues left in UKIP.

Those old colleagues on the other side of the split had held firm to UKIP's original premise, electing a more credible and media-friendly leader in Nigel Farage and, during the mayoral campaign, welcoming their first MP – the Tory defector Bob Spink. Gerard Batten, the candidate in 2008 and a founder member of the party in 1993, was an MEP who had developed a certain profile through his annual audit of how much the European Parliament costs the UK. An affable former BT salesman, he had known Aleksandr Litvinenko, the former Russian spy who was poisoned in London. He ran a traditional conservative campaign focusing on crime, tax and immigration.

Still, UKIP's chances this time were a good deal worse than they had been in 2004. There were no European elections and it looked as though many of the right-wing voters from 2004 would instead back the British National Party, which made its candidate, Richard Barnbrook, a more central figure. One of the eleven BNP councillors elected to Barking & Dagenham Council in 2006, Barnbrook has worked as an artist and art teacher and was engaged to Simone Clarke, a former ballerina with the English National Ballet who had backed the BNP. His argument that 'parts of our capital city are coming to resemble a dangerous and grotty third-world town' undoubtedly resonated with some voters, but the other parties shunned him.

Three other candidates completed the field. The one with the highest profile was the English Democrat, Matt O'Connor. The party had initially expected to put up the former *Sun* television columnist Gary Bushell but he withdrew and O'Connor, with his proven capacity for generating column inches, outrage and debate as the founder of campaigning group Fathers4Justice (F4J), proved an attractive alternative. With O'Connor at the helm F4J members had carried out some striking protests: appearing as Spiderman on a crane above Tower Bridge, throwing a condom full of purple flour at Tony Blair during Prime Minister's Questions and even sending Batman onto the balcony of Buckingham Palace. An interesting political figure (he had previously been a member of the Fabians and CND and claimed to have campaigned for Cherie Blair when she stood for Parliament in 1983), O'Connor promised to run a vigorous, populist campaign against the tax system, which he claimed badly disadvantaged the English. He tried to withdraw from the campaign with a week to go, citing disagreements with the party and frustration that he had not been able to get more publicity. By that time the ballot papers had already been printed and the deposit had been paid, though, and all he could do was save himself the hassle of another week's campaigning.

Running a less populist but more firmly rooted campaign was Alan Craig, the Christian Choice candidate and a councillor representing the Christian Peoples Alliance (CPA) on Newham Council. Elected there in 2002, the only non-Labour councillor, he automatically became the official opposition and in 2004 became the party's leader. Although the CPA had come fourth in the last mayoral election, as with several of the other candidates Craig's main role was to raise the profile of his party for the Assembly elections. They had high hopes for success: the CPA had come close to winning a seat on the London Assembly in 2000.

The final candidate, and the only independent in the race, was

Winston McKenzie. McKenzie ran another populist campaign, albeit one which managed not to be terribly popular. Aiming to become the first black Mayor of London, his campaign was in many ways the least explicable: he wasn't using it to raise issues like O'Connor, he couldn't win, and he wasn't using it as a way of raising the profile of candidates running for the London Assembly (since he was an independent). The former champion boxer was a colourful character and certainly relished a political fight, too, having been involved with both Labour and the Conservatives; he had even been – briefly – spokesman on sport for Veritas.

The cast of ten who ran for Mayor certainly contained more than enough personalities, yet at various points it looked as though at least five other candidates, including two big names, might have joined. The smaller fish were Dennis Delderfield, representing New Britain, John Flunder for the Senior Citizens Party and Chris Prior for the Stop Congestion Charging Party. The first big name was John Bird, the social entrepreneur and founder of the *Big Issue*. He flirted with the Conservatives first, then contemplated an independent bid, but pulled back to focus on a campaign against poverty. Second was Michael Hodges, editor-at-large for the weekly listings magazine *Time Out*. Hodges's weekly column was the Marmite of the publishing world – the letters page demonstrated how people either loved it or loathed it. Readers of all stripes responded to his mayoral campaign, though, and the magazine was able to put forward a manifesto for what Londoners wanted (including special planning protections along the Thames, more involvement for Londoners in the Olympics and a pedestrian charter for London). It even held its own hustings, but Hodges himself withdrew from the contest just as nominations were closing. *Time Out* claimed that it had raised the necessary £10,000 and garnered the necessary signatures from every part of London for Hodges to stand, but withdrew because it had accomplished its main aim – to show how hard it was for ordinary Londoners to get into the race, to make a mark on London politics. Hodges added that for him a prime motivating factor was his capacity to draw support from Ken Livingstone in such a close race: he was standing aside to 'save this city from rule by a toff, I suppose,' he said.

The *Time Out* campaign highlighted the difficulties any ordinary Londoner would have getting into the race. If a magazine with the resources of *Time Out* struggled, imagine what it would be like for a normal citizen: not only getting all those signatures but raising £10,000 – and in reality far more for the campaigning and publicity budget. In many ways it is not just the requirements to qualify which present a hurdle to ordinary people getting involved; the process does, too. By only allowing the top two candidates through to the final round, the votes cast for minor candidates are effectively discarded and only those voters' second preferences counted. Unfortunately, by inviting only the four leading candidates to its own hustings *Time Out* did rather damage its claim to moral superiority, and it turned its campaign to Parliament, promoting a House of Commons motion to relax the qualification requirements. More harmful than all this to all the minor candidates, though – and indeed everyone other than Boris Johnson himself – was what many regarded as the *Evening Standard*'s campaign for Boris. The minor candidates complained that the newspaper's apparent desire to see Boris in City Hall meant they got pretty short shrift, although they would still pop up regularly during the campaign and pitch in ideas which enlivened the race.

2007: Sowing the seeds

Once Boris Johnson was in place as Conservative candidate, the seven-month battle could begin between him and the man he had previously branded 'King Newt' – but whom he would later cheekily refer to in speeches as 'Mayor Leaving-soon'. However, the contest had effectively started as soon as Boris announced his intention to seek the Conservative nomination, since all observers could foresee no outcome but a thundering Boris victory in the Tory primary.

In early August 2007, Ken admitted that Boris would be 'the most formidable opponent I will face in my political career' in an interview for Radio 4's *Today* programme, describing him as 'a charming and engaging rogue'. But he said he was keen to stop the Ken-v-Boris contest becoming a battle of personalities, claiming: 'I want to get onto the policy ... This is not a sort of "Celebrity Big Mayor", it's a serious issue about how you run the city.'

But very quickly the personal attacks on Boris began to emerge, initially centring on his attitudes to ethnic minorities. Doreen Lawrence, the mother of Stephen Lawrence, the black teenager murdered in 1993, declared Boris to be 'not an appropriate person to run a multicultural city like London', referring to articles he had written at the time of the Macpherson report on her son's death. 'Those people that think he is a lovable rogue need to take a good look at themselves, and look at him. I just find his remarks very offensive.

I think once people read his views, there is no way he is going to get the support of any people in the black community.' Writing about the Macpherson report as a columnist, Boris had seized on, among other things, what he described as a 'weird recommendation' to criminalise racist statements or behaviour occurring in private. 'Not even under the law of Ceauşescu's Romania could you be prosecuted for what you said in your own kitchen,' he had stated. He had concluded that 'what started as a sensible attempt to find justice for the family of Stephen Lawrence has given way to hysteria.' A spokesman for Boris insisted that he 'loathes racism in any form and this is evident if the wealth of articles he has written on the death of Stephen Lawrence and the subsequent Macpherson report are looked at in their entirety.'

But a black Labour MP, Dawn Butler, also waded into the row, highlighting a reference he had made in a 2002 article to 'flag-waving piccaninnies' and the 'watermelon smiles' of tribal warriors when the Queen visited Commonwealth countries. 'These are disgraceful comments that shame Boris Johnson and shame the Conservative Party,' said Butler. 'No-one with such views can be the mayor of a city with the largest black population in Britain.'

The attacks continued throughout August, Ken's supporters having meticulously combed through all Boris's writing over the years to find things he had written which had the potential to cause him problems now he was running for such a high-profile role. Indeed, the left-wing group Compass published a dossier of things he had said over the years which it felt would alarm London voters, ranging from support for the Iraq War and opposition to the minimum wage to comments which could be deemed as sexist and offensive to black people or homosexuals.

His opponents would return to these various allegations regularly throughout the campaign, and Boris seemed uncomfortable whenever they were raised, not least because quotes would be thrown at him that were taken completely out of context. He certainly appeared unkeen ever to enter into discussions about these matters, although at a debate in early 2008 he would apologise for the language he had used in the 2002 article for which Butler had condemned him.

No sooner had Boris been announced as the mayoral candidate than he was on his way to Blackpool for the Conservative Party conference, where he would address the gathering in the Winter Gardens. He was given a hero's welcome and delivered an eight-minute speech in which he tackled head on the suggestion that he was not a serious candidate. 'When people ask me "are you serious about this", I can tell them that I can think of nothing more serious than the security and prosperity of the powerhouse of the British economy, whose booming service industries are the best possible vindication of the revolutions brought in by Conservative governments.' But he also signalled that he would not immediately be announcing detailed plans; rather, he would be spending a few months crunching the numbers, looking into what powers he would have and how he could wield them.

Boris was cheered to the rafters, although he had not impressed absolutely everybody. Arnold Schwarzenegger, the Governor of California, was due to follow him by delivering a message to the conference live by satellite from the United States. Footage later emerged of the former film star listening to Boris's speech as he waited to say his piece, in which he was clearly unimpressed with the mayoral candidate's unique style. 'This guy is fumbling all over the place,' a bemused Schwarzenegger whispered to his aides off camera.

As the conference came to an end, speculation was rife that a general election was about to be called. This presented Boris with a dilemma: would he step down from Parliament to make way for a new Conservative candidate in Henley and show that he was concentrating his efforts on the mayoral election? Or would he plump for the default Boris option of having his cake and eating it? Unsurprisingly, he seemed to opt for the latter plan of action, telling the *Oxford Mail*: 'If they [Henley Conservative Association] would like me to run, I'm not going to let them down.' Labour seized on this, with a spokesman immediately claiming that this demonstrated a 'lack of seriousness in wanting to be Mayor of London' on Boris's part. Yet the question became academic when Gordon Brown finally ended the speculation on Saturday 6 October and signalled that he would not be going to the country. One early commitment Boris did make, however, was to give up alcohol for the duration of the campaign, which led to him losing more than a stone and a half in weight and feeling fitter than he had done in years.

Boris took offices in County Hall, the old headquarters of the defunct Greater London Council, and his campaign was to be headed by Dan Ritterband, who had previously worked for Michael Howard and Saatchi & Saatchi. He had also been involved in David Cameron's campaign for the Conservative leadership and was running Nick Boles's stalled bid for the mayoral nomination before throwing his lot in with Boris. Other early recruits to the campaign were a media team in the form of Katie Perrior and Jo Tanner, former press officers at Conservative Campaign Headquarters (CCHQ) who had set up their own PR company. Dubbed 'the Trinny and Susannah of political PR' by Michael White of the *Guardian*, they were well known among political journalists but also tough operators when they needed to be and would be described as 'the women who have to keep Boris out of mischief' by the *Evening Standard*.

There then followed a period of self-imposed purdah, during which Boris had to read himself into the role, although he did allow himself to make the odd policy statement during November and early December to add to the few pledges he had made during the primary race, such as scrapping bendy buses and replacing them with a new version of the traditional Routemaster. Speaking to the National House-Building Council he indicated that he was sympathetic to the idea of relaxing the target that 50 per cent of new homes should be 'affordable' and in late November he announced that he would create what would become the Mayor's Fund. Live CCTV screening on buses would be trialled and he also made a renewed effort to rebut accusations of racism by launching an attack on the British National Party and tabling an early day motion in the Commons calling on all parties to 'work together to combat anyone who seeks to play the race card'. He wrote a piece in the *Evening Standard* before Christmas in which he lamented the increase in youth crime and indicated his desire to increase the number of mobile knife scanners in use. He also took the opportunity to laud the work that Ray Lewis was doing with Afro-Caribbean boys from disadvantaged backgrounds at the Eastside Young Leaders Academy – an early reference to the man who would become Deputy Mayor, his first appointment after winning the election.

Yet talk of Boris winning seemed fanciful at that stage, even to some of those closest to the campaign. A series of London Tories were being taken in to give him masterclasses in the dynamics of London politics, the nuts and bolts of how the Assembly works and the powers of the Mayor – and by all accounts he was learning fast. However, he was still busy with other media commitments and seemed far from 100 per cent committed to the mayoral bid. Eyebrows were also raised in some sections of the generally Republican-inclined Conservative Party when he endorsed Hillary Clinton's bid for the US presidency in his *Daily Telegraph* column.

There were increasingly serious concerns inside CCHQ and David Cameron's office that the campaign was suffering from a sense of drift and lacking in professionalism and money. Cameron himself had even remarked that 'inside Boris there is a serious, ambitious politician fighting to get out', in a thinly veiled admission of his personal frustration with the way things were going. 'Boris had thus far coasted through life on the back of his charm and charisma, but that alone was not going to be enough to win an election against Ken Livingstone,' was how another confidant summed up the situation. 'I'm sure there were nights when he must have woken up in a cold sweat and thought: "How the hell am I going to talk my way out of this?"'

Ritterband had his creative talents, but no experience of actually running a campaign on this scale or raising the necessary funds to do so. In the words of one who was closely involved, 'Dan didn't understand his own strengths and weaknesses and was frankly out of his depth'. There was no sense of a cohesive structure or a co-ordinated effort. Some in the party thought that CCHQ should take over the operation, but Boris was insistent that it remain independent – not least because he felt that the party machine had worked against his best interests before, for example over his trip to apologise to Liverpool. Yet with alarm bells ringing and fears growing that Boris's candidacy could turn into a disaster, it was evident that something had to be done, and Shadow Chancellor George Osborne hauled Boris into his office to tell him as much.

The first crucial recruit to the effort to turn things around was Lord Marland, the multi-millionaire businessman and former treasurer of the Conservative Party, who is well connected in both the party and the City. Having raised in the region of £75 million during his time as party treasurer, he was tasked with building up a campaign war chest of £1.5 million or so, which he would manage with some ease, without taking more than £50,000 from any individual. Fundraising efforts included two £1,000-a-ticket dinners, one of which raised a figure approaching £250,000. Among those who donated were Sir Cameron Mackintosh, Sir Tim Rice and Lord Laidlaw, who during the campaign would check into a South African clinic to be treated for sex addiction. But arguably Marland's most pivotal role was, along with Osborne, to persuade Lynton Crosby, the Australian political strategist, to come to London and take over the running of the campaign. His appointment was secured in the week leading up to Christmas and he set about salvaging the lacklustre campaign as soon as he began work in early January.

Crosby, nicknamed 'the wizard of Oz', had masterminded four election victories in his homeland for John Howard but was no stranger to British politics. He had been brought in to run the Conservatives' 2005 general election campaign, during which time he had forged good links at the top of the party, gaining a number of friends with whom he would touch base whenever business brought him to London. Aside from the benefit in him being a master strategist, he was someone who would pose no threat to Boris, since he would come in, do his stuff, and then return to Australia once it was all over. As it turned out, he was worth every penny of the £140,000 he cost for the four months he was in London.

A second figure brought in to bolster the campaign and give it further solidity was another Australian, James McGrath. A former chief of staff to Francis Maude who had latterly been working as an adviser to Osborne, he would play a vital role in supporting Crosby and as a link man to the party HQ. Ritterband – although effectively demoted – was said by those around him initially to have felt relief at having a burden removed from his shoulders. He did remain heavily involved in the campaign but concentrated his efforts on areas such as marketing and liaison with interest groups, which is where his skills were best deployed.

Other key players central to the team were: Alex Crowley, an ex-staffer for the Conservatives at City Hall, who oversaw research and policy; Ian Clement, the leader of Bexley Council, who provided links with GLA members and councillors; Ed Staite, a CCHQ press officer who latterly joined Perrior and Tanner on the media team; and Paul Clarke, another former Saatchi & Saatchi man who worked on communications and marketing. (Clement would stand down from Bexley Council after the election to become Deputy Mayor for Government Relations.) In addition, once a schedule of daily meetings kicked in, these figures would usually be joined by the Opposition Chief Whip in the House of Commons, Patrick McLoughlin, or one of his colleagues, as a way of ensuring the parliamentary party was kept in the loop and that a good relationship existed with the Tory MPs.

Crosby hit the ground running. His first task was to inject a much-needed sense of discipline into the campaign – and into Boris himself. Whilst he is bright, charming, personable and ambitious, self-discipline had never been his forte. He had a reputation for being late, underprepared and generally flying by the seat of his pants, which was simply not going to do if he was to mount a serious campaign. Friends of Boris report that he appeared to undergo a Damascene conversion on this front after conversations with Crosby – a man who does not mince his words – over the Christmas and New Year break.

There was also the question of his appearance. He virtually revelled in his semi-shambolic look and had previously been known on occasion to have purposely ruffled his mop of hair before appearing in front of an audience. Campaign insiders insist that there was no makeover as such, but that he did accept that he needed to buy some better suits and get a modest haircut, which he did willingly. Whilst the media read far more into the significance of those measures than campaign chiefs felt was necessary, they did go some way to demonstrating that he was committed to the job and taking it seriously.

Having smartened himself up, he was then, believe it or not, subjected to media training. It may come as a surprise to learn that someone who has worked in the media his entire life underwent such a process, and Boris himself did not see the need for it and resisted. But journalists do not automatically make good communicators and persuaders, he was told, and whilst his inimitable style won him plaudits on *Have I Got News for You* and as an after-dinner speaker, it was not deemed to be best suited for the televised debates in which he would go up against his rivals for the mayoralty. There were only two sessions of media training, but they were nonetheless important in helping him hone his message into television-friendly soundbites. 'I bloody needed that,' Boris told his team afterwards. Towards the end of the campaign Crosby would sometimes turn up with Boris to his more important media appearances and provide last-minute coaching and encouragement.

Crosby's most important job, however, was to devise and execute a strategy which would get voters to put their cross in Boris's box come 1 May. And the strategy had five prongs to it: firstly, to get people voting (for Boris) in outer London, outside Underground zones 1 and 2, who had not voted in the mayoral elections in 2000 and 2004; secondly, to motivate existing Conservatives to vote for Boris; thirdly, to persuade voters, especially those in inner London who don't usually vote Conservative, to switch to Boris this time; fourthly, to suppress Labour's vote, particularly in its strongest areas, even if it just meant Labour voters staying at home rather than switching; and fifthly, to go after Liberal Democrat voters, persuading them that their candidate couldn't win and that Boris was worth at least a second preference.

As regards the first two prongs, media reports talked of a 'doughnut strategy' in which the campaign was chasing votes virtually exclusively in the outer London boroughs, but the reality was more complicated

than that. There was ward-by-ward data from the 2004 mayoral
election and the 2006 borough elections to pore over and make con-
clusions as to which were strongest for the Conservatives. And of the
625 electoral wards across the capital, 329 were designated as Boris's
(and the Conservatives') most fruitful areas, where he could win the
election. Whilst for some of the outlying boroughs, such as Bromley,
nearly every ward was included among the 329, there were nonetheless wards being targeted from every single borough. Indeed,
Westminster, Kensington & Chelsea, Hammersmith & Fulham and
Wandsworth were all deemed to include a lot of extremely Boris-
friendly territory and were far from being outer London boroughs.

As for Boris himself, he already had a public profile, which was
essential for an election of this kind, and generally provoked a positive reaction from voters, which was also a fantastic advantage. His
challenge, however, was to show that he wanted the job, that he was
up to the job and what he would do with the job if elected.

Crosby would oversee the writing of all campaign literature, all of
which was highly targeted and crafted to deliver different 'below the
line' messages in different areas, in accordance with the strategy out-
lined above. In Ken's strongest areas, the message would be honed to
suppress the Labour vote, in a number of cases not mentioning Boris
at all. In areas where the Liberal Democrats traditionally did well, the
aim was to demonstrate that Boris was the only viable alternative to
Ken and, if nothing else, to court those second-preference votes.
Meanwhile, in areas best for the Conservatives, the message was all
about ensuring that those people did vote, on the basis that it genuinely would make a difference. In fact there would be a total of 397
different pieces of literature delivered across the capital by Boris supporters over the course of the campaign. All those efforts were backed
up with activity in call centres from where volunteers would do
telephone canvassing, in addition to the traditional door-to-door

campaigning on the ground, as they sought to get out the vote.

Incidentally, it should be noted that there is something of a question mark as to whether Boris himself really believed he could win at the outset. In the open letter to the people of Henley he would write in the *Henley Standard* in May 2008, he stated:

> When I set out on my mission to unseat Ken Livingstone more than nine months ago, there were all kinds of risks. There was a considerable risk that I would be thrashed by the Great Newt. And then there was a risk that I would win ... At the time, I have to admit, it seemed a pretty small risk.

Whether or not that was a literary flourish, if he did genuinely wonder whether it could be done, any doubts were vanquished once Crosby was on the scene.

But under no circumstances would Crosby tolerate any premature triumphalism, and anyone who took a single Tory vote for granted got short shrift. Yes, the campaign needed momentum, but it was essential to the strategy that the Conservative voters they were targeting saw the election as being down to the wire so that they would feel that their vote was essential to the effort.

All the while, Ken was busy running London. During the latter half of 2007, policies began to emerge which would set the scene for the election campaign proper. In August, for example, he announced the consultation on charging owners of vehicles in vehicle excise duty band G – which includes the most polluting cars – £25 a day to enter the congestion charging zone. He said that he was keeping 'an open mind' on the proposals until he had considered the responses to the consultation, although it was pretty clear that it was a policy he favoured and it would indeed eventually form a central plank of his manifesto. Then, perhaps anticipating a similar proposal from bicycling Boris, he announced that he was considering a cycle hire scheme similar to the one operating in Paris, which would allow travellers to pick up and drop off bikes from street corners located around the city.

In September Ken announced a three-year plan to build 50,000 more affordable homes by 2011, doubling the supply of homes for social rent, and at the Labour Party conference later that month, he announced that tenders would be invited early in the New Year to 'retro-fit' every public building in London, with the aim of reducing their carbon emissions by at least 25 per cent. He even managed a public show of unity there with the newly ensconced Prime Minister, Gordon Brown, with whom he had endured frosty relations for some years.

The following month, the £16 billion Crossrail project – which would see trains running across London from 2017 – at last got the green light after the Corporation of London agreed to meet a final funding gap of £350 million. Ken hailed it as the most important transport scheme he had sought to deliver. 'Crossrail is not just a transport scheme – it is the key to the next twenty years of economic development of London,' he said. There was also confirmation in October that Ken, who had already been reselected as Labour's mayoral candidate in May, would be allowed to run for a third term in office. During the 2006/07 parliamentary session, the Lords passed an amendment to the Greater London Authority Bill – clearly targeted at Ken – limiting any individual from serving more than two terms as Mayor. When the bill returned to the Commons, the amendment was rejected by all parties without a vote and the Lords subsequently backed down in its attempt to prevent Ken from running again.

In November, Ken strutted his stuff on the international stage as he took an 85-strong delegation on a week-long trip to India – at an estimated cost of £750,000 – where he opened two new London offices in Delhi and Mumbai. These offices, nicknamed 'Kenbassies' by some of his opponents, would 'operate as a gateway not just for encouraging trade and inward investment into the city but to promote London as a key destination for tourists and students,' he said.

But back in London, the storm clouds were about to start gathering over Lee Jasper, Ken's long-time friend and his director of equalities and policing. On 5 December, Andrew Gilligan wrote the first of many pieces in the *Evening Standard* about Jasper, which would ultimately lead to his resignation three months later, causing considerable damage to the image of Ken's administration in the process.

The son of a Jamaican father and a white mother who brought him up on her own in Oldham, Jasper had long been involved in what detractors would describe as 'the race relations industry'. Immediately before joining Ken's administration in 2000, he had spent five years as director of the 1990 Trust, an organisation promoting social, economic and political rights for black and ethnic minority communities. In the words of a GLA press release in 2001, he was 'the foremost black expert on police and black community relationships' and, as a member of Ken's advisory cabinet, he advised him on policing and race relations matters. Yet he had remained chairman of a number of other groups and committees, including the National Black Alliance, the National Black Caucus and Operation Black Vote, and was national secretary of the National Assembly Against Racism. And it was his close links to so many outside organisations which would eventually bring about his downfall.

Gilligan reported that Jasper was under investigation for channelling up to £2.5 million from the Mayor's office and the London Development Agency to organisations 'controlled by himself, his friends and his business associates' which appeared 'to do little or no work in return'. The report stated:

One grant recipient, Diversity International, controlled by a long-standing friend and business associate of Mr Jasper, Joel O'Loughlin, received £295,000 in LDA funding for the Diversity Dividend, a web-based tool for London business, even though the business consultancy has no expertise in computers and is based in Liverpool. The website does not exist, the company has now gone into liquidation and all the money paid to it has vanished … Another project, Brixton Base, whose patron is Mr Jasper and whose director is Errol Walters, another friend, has received £287,000 from the LDA over the past two years for premises even though it has occupied an LDA-owned building throughout that time and was charged no rent in the first year … Mr Walters is also acting director of the Black Londoners' Forum, based in the same building as Brixton Base, which has received at least a further £291,000 directly from the Mayor. The *Standard* has seen the official funding agreement for £53,000 of this money which imposes extraordinarily few obligations on the Black Londoners' Forum in return for its grant. The agreement says that in return for the BLF's money all the campaigning it has to do is support an online petition against attacks on asylum seekers. This currently contains 97 signatures. The BLF's real function appears to be to offer enthusiastic support for the Mayor. Its website republishes mayoral press releases word-for-word as its own and it responds to mayoral consultations with glowing praise of his policies. This is then cited by Mr Livingstone as evidence that his policies are supported by the black community.

The article went on to make a string of similar allegations about other organisations and claimed that a GLA inquiry was being conducted by its chief executive, Anthony Mayer. Both the LDA and Ken's office refused to answer questions from the *Evening Standard* about the funding of the organisations, whilst Jasper insisted that he did not get involved in grant funding decisions. 'This is an attempt to smear a well-known and respected community activist,' responded Ken, who branded the article a 'tissue of lies' made up of 'smears and innuendos'. Two days later, further questions were raised when Gilligan revealed that despite earning £117,000 a year, Jasper was renting a housing association property in Clapham for a mere £90 a week.

Gilligan's assault continued on 11 December, with a report that in the fortnight since the allegations were put to Ken and the LDA, they had still failed to answer any specific questions. He wrote that whilst the organisations at the centre of the allegations had encouraged supporters to protest to the *Standard* about the paper's 'outrageous slurs on them', he had been cheered by 'a greater proportion of calls, emails and letters from the black community thanking us for our work and – more importantly – offering extremely useful new information'.

Ken then revealed that the LDA would be carrying out an investigation into the funds awarded to the Brixton Base project, although he used a press conference to attack the *Evening Standard* coverage, calling Gilligan the most discredited reporter in Britain. But more allegations followed. On 13 December Gilligan published the details of leaked emails which showed that Manny Lewis, the chief executive of the LDA, expressed 'the deepest possible concern' about a £345,000 grant to O'Loughlin. Gilligan wrote:

> The emails obtained by the *Standard* show that Mr Jasper's friend, Joel O'Loughlin, grossly overcharged, deceived the LDA and failed to provide any of the services

he promised. The LDA chief executive, Manny Lewis, wanted to sack Mr O'Loughlin, claw back all the LDA's money and even talked about suing him. But within days, after Mr O'Loughlin contacted Mr Jasper, the LDA performed a 180-degree turn, offering Mr O'Loughlin another £250,000 and a lucrative consultancy. Two senior LDA managers who vehemently protested against this deal, one calling it 'extortionate' and 'against the interests of the GLA', were subsequently sacked. The emails show that Mr Jasper played the decisive role in one of the sackings.

This latest chapter in the saga prompted Ken to call for Gilligan to be sacked for waging a 'dirty and mendacious campaign', but the *Evening Standard*'s editor, Veronica Wadley, declared him to be 'an outstanding and fearless journalist who has our full support to pursue investigations that are in the public interest'. Even if Boris was not yet firing on all cylinders, Andrew Gilligan certainly was.

When Brian Paddick finally joined the fray in mid-November, his first act was to call for the resignation of his old boss, Sir Ian Blair, the Metropolitan Police Commissioner, whose position, he said, was becoming 'increasingly untenable'. 'I, reluctantly, am coming to the view that London would be better off without Ian Blair as Commissioner,' he said. Earlier in the month, the Met had been found guilty of a series of errors and endangering the public over the fatal shooting of Jean Charles de Menezes at Stockwell Tube station in July 2005. Despite the judge branding it a 'corporate failure', Blair would not budge and he still enjoyed the confidence of both Ken and the Home Secretary, Jacqui Smith. Boris, incidentally, had also concluded that his position was 'clearly untenable'.

Most of Paddick's pronouncements over the following weeks

related to the issue of policing – as he hoped that his experience as a senior police officer would persuade the public that this made him worth voting for. He again attacked Blair, over the perception that he was too close to the Labour Government. 'It calls the political independence of the police into question,' he told the *Daily Telegraph*. 'If there's a perception that their chief is aligned to a political party, that undermines the rank-and-file officers.'

He later pledged to make the Met a more comfortable place for ethnic minorities to work, and also announced that he favoured a review of the western extension to the congestion charge zone. Paddick also demonstrated his radical side by calling for the Queen to be stripped of many of her constitutional powers and for the role of the monarchy to be 'largely ceremonial'.

Paddick's initial tactic of portraying himself as the only serious alternative to Ken led to a highly critical assessment of Boris in an end-of-year interview with epolitix.com. 'Boris has got into the habit of believing that nobody will like him unless he makes a joke,' he said. 'At the end of the day he just can't help cracking jokes and quite often they're offensive to the people that he's making the joke about and we need a serious ambassador for London to be our Mayor – not a clown.' He also called into question Boris's motive for giving up alcohol for the campaign. 'Clearly Boris is under strict orders not to be himself and clearly once you have had a drink or two you tend to become more yourself than if you haven't had a drink, you let your defences come down and the true you comes out.'

Yet whilst Boris did allow himself a glass of bubbly during Christmas festivities, the card he sent out carried a prescient message: 'I wish you all a merry Christmas and a happy new Mayor'.

January: Under way at last

With the New Year the campaign began to gather pace, a YouGov poll for ITV's *London Tonight* suggesting a dramatic narrowing of the race. Putting Ken Livingstone on 45 per cent, Boris Johnson on 44 per cent and Brian Paddick on just 7 per cent, it showed that each still had hurdles to leap. Ken was clearly being damaged by the growing crisis over cronyism in his office and at the London Development Agency; Paddick had yet to persuade voters that he was a credible alternative; and Boris had yet to demonstrate the passion, commitment and seriousness which many voters regarded as the prerequisite for the job. For Boris, though, this poll was the first concrete demonstration that he could win: after what he described as a 'crap' campaign up to that point (for which he blamed himself, having spent much of the previous year out of the country filming), to come within a point of Ken clearly showed it was all to play for. The rhetorical fireworks were soon being let off as the candidates began to clash over the Mayor's record, and what the challengers would do differently.

The first issue of substance was the buses. A 'more in sorrow than anger' opinion piece by Nick Cohen in the *Evening Standard* concluded that whilst 'the revival of the bus network has been Hendy [Peter Hendy, head of Transport for London] and Ken Livingstone's greatest achievement in public office [...] both men seem indifferent to their passengers'. He described the incredulity on the faces of free-riding bus passengers when he actually swiped his Oyster card to pay on one of the bendy buses, and demanded that TfL do something about rampant fare evasion. Then Boris went on the offensive, accusing Ken of 'serial dishonesty' over fares, which had risen well above inflation in recent years, including a 3.8 per cent rise that month. Ken blamed the train companies, since he had frozen single Tube and bus Oyster fares for 2008, and said the other above-inflation rises went on repaying the interest on loans taken out for investment in the Tube.

As Ken came under attack for parts of his record, on another front one calculated political appeal appeared to be bearing fruit. The *Guardian* website published a letter from sixty-three Muslim community leaders backing him for another term in office. 'He has stood out in support of a multicultural society and has supported the Muslim communities of the city against racism and Islamophobia,' they wrote. The letter caused a minor stir, with some of the signatories later criticised by the Charity Commission because they signed in their official capacity as leaders of groups whose charitable status prohibited such political activity. It was a minor skirmish, but Ken would face questions about pandering to Muslim groups throughout the campaign, especially when it emerged that some of the more controversial individuals he had embraced were actively drumming up support in mosques and Muslim community centres across London.

Meanwhile, outside the campaign, the horror of teenage murders in London rolled on. By the end of the first week of January, two had been killed already, and Boris had entered the fray. This kind of issue is very difficult for opposition politicians – they cannot be seen to be making political capital whilst a family is grieving, but they cannot be silent on such a massive issue, either. So when Boris was penning his piece for the *Standard*, he had to maintain a delicate balance. Predictably, he attacked Ken for his failure to act. 'It is a scandal,' he wrote, arguing that it was all very well to blame social changes but 'we can't just keep turning the pages of our papers in search of brighter news'. His solution was part traditional Conservative law and order, and part community based. He name-checked several of the most prominent voluntary organisations working with young people and promised a more engaged approach from a Johnson administration in City Hall. This appeal to the charitable and voluntary sector may have been an old-fashioned Conservative notion in many ways, but it fitted with what the Conservatives were promoting at a national level. As importantly for Boris's campaign, it fitted very neatly with the stories in the *Standard* about waste at the LDA. It was hard not to be struck by the subtext here: why is so much LDA cash going to groups who don't seem to deliver, when there are so many great organisations out there achieving incredible things?

Very shortly, Boris would get the chance to challenge Ken on all these issues as the three candidates came face to face on television for the first time on ITV's *London Talking* programme. But before the debate the candidates started winding one another up, trying to gain an advantage in the psychological game. In what would become a regular part of their pre-debate routine they would, like Vegas boxers, do and say things intended to psychologically discomfort their opponents. Ken began: this was, he said, 'the first time I've been able to pin Boris Johnson down to one [a debate]. I'm really looking forward to it and I'm sure Londoners are looking forward to it.' He said he thought he and Brian Paddick would likely agree on 90 per cent of things, with Boris lonely, no-one sharing his arguments. And on Paddick? 'I like him. I think he wouldn't be a bad Mayor at all. But he has got to look for points of difference with me.' Boris responded as only Boris could: 'Bring it on, bring it on, you big girl's blouse, that's what I say.'

The debate itself was the first opportunity for a mass audience to see any real fire from the contenders. And fire there was – Boris showcasing a new assertiveness, aggressiveness even, as he challenged the

Mayor on rising crime and the spate of teenage murders: the Mayor must 'get a grip on this problem ... it breaks my heart to see so many kids growing up scared, and so many adults scared of kids'. Ken was also aggressive, forcefully putting his argument that 'no Mayor, no commissioner of police, can stop youngsters killing each other if they haven't been given the moral code that my parents gave my generation'. He blamed 'horrendous levels of glamorised violence in cinemas and on TV. This is the generation whose parents grew up in the 80s – get your snout in the trough and it doesn't matter a damn about anyone else ... You've got to get back to those shared values,' he argued. Boris and Paddick were both to use this argument for the rest of the campaign to make their case that Ken wasn't serious about tackling crime, Boris adding that it was 'tragic' to blame these problems on what happened thirty years ago. He was strong on other issues, too, and he was funny – when Ken said he would be 'a disastrous Mayor' Boris immediately shot back: 'I think you're already a disastrous Mayor.' But Boris was also disorganised and clearly hadn't yet mastered his brief. His answers about bus conductors and why he didn't seem to have expressed much interest in London until now were a masterclass in bluff and bluster. By contrast Paddick came across well – serious, on top of the brief. Ken was confident and pugilistic – not at all afraid to get stuck in. Almost his first sentence was the premise of his whole campaign: 'If you don't believe that London's improved over the last eight years then don't vote for me.' And answering a question about the western extension to the congestion charge, he seemed to accept that at least one group thought exactly that: 'The people that are living in the zone will have the added benefit that, if I decide to sign the order to make the £25 for the most polluting vehicles, the air quality of the air they breathe will so improve they'll live longer and carry on voting against me.' Yet for all this it was Boris's night. He spoke eloquently and with some passion about some of the most difficult issues; he dismissed others skilfully. He would have to cut down the waffle and improve his answers to other questions, but there was plenty of time for that before the voters really started tuning in.

The next news was an attempt from Camp Ken to get the campaign back on track: they had hired the advertising firm behind the Dairy Milk gorillas as part of a £400,000 communications effort. Yet the clouds of Lee Jasper-related gloom were now gathering ominously over Ken's campaign. For every piece of good news – on 11 January Jasper was cleared by the LDA of interfering behaviour in funding awards – came something seemingly much worse – the LDA referred to the police three projects which it had funded. And more came from the *Standard*: the LDA probe was not a 'report of the outside auditors' which Ken had claimed it to be, reported Andrew Gilligan, but an internal review led by an LDA official. It was these dismissive responses to the stories which were to damage Ken as much as the stories themselves. Many people (including Gilligan himself) were amazed that Ken didn't just set up a proper inquiry to kick this story into the long grass until after the election, but he didn't. A week later Gilligan had found a London MP from each major party to support his case, and at a London Assembly hearing the LDA chief executive and chief financial officer further undermined the case that the inquiry had been independent.* The Labour MP Kate Hoey, who would reappear several times during the campaign, also wrote to Gordon Brown to express her concerns about Ken.

Yet the gathering clouds were not just linked to Jasper. Martin Bright, the political editor of the left-wing political magazine the *New Statesman*, had conducted a six-month investigation for a

---

* The MPs were Lynne Featherstone (Liberal Democrat), Greg Hands (Conservative) and Kate Hoey (Labour).

Dispatches documentary on Channel 4, looking into how Ken had run his office. Parts of it leaked early, but Bright himself gave a preview of the full report in that week's *New Statesman*. He claimed that Ken regularly drank whisky at Mayor's Questions, and on one occasion had done so at a People's Questions at Ilford town hall. This, Bright said, breached the Greater London Authority's rules about drinking and he felt it showed 'a degree of disrespect' to the public audience. Ken had even said within hearing of one of the Channel 4 team that 'he needed a whisky to get him through Mayor's Questions. He added that this was because of a cough.' Aside from this, Bright declared himself 'surprised' at the Mayor's response to the leaks about his allegations. That response had certainly been vigorous: Ken complained that Channel 4 was guilty of an undue attempt to influence the electoral process, and said that Bright and his team had 'spent a year preparing the documentary, interviewing all my enemies, it's going to be all dramatic music and gloomy shadows and all they're offering me is the chance they'll flash up a sentence saying "I don't believe a word of it" on the back.' If this reflected Ken's ruthless streak, his response to the claims about drinking was vintage Ken the showman: 'I don't think I've ever reached Winston Churchill's levels, and as it didn't impair him in the destruction of the greatest evil facing humanity, it won't interfere with my continuing to lead Londoners to the sunny uplands of the future.' He told LBC's Nick Ferrari that 'I should imagine I get a couple of glasses of wine down me at any reception – I suspect I most probably drink about half of what I did when I was an MP. A couple of bottles of wine a week in total. I'd like to drink a lot more!'

When the full programme was finally shown the following week it contained much more serious accusations than those about the drinking. In particular, it alleged that during the 2004 campaign his staff had been working on the campaign when they were being paid by the GLA; that Ken used GLA funds to pay for a character assassi-nation of Trevor Phillips, the chairman-designate of the Commission for Equality and Human Rights; that the LDA, 'Ken's piggybank', was misdirecting money; that the congestion charge had not done much to tackle congestion; that Ken's PR budget had been excessively large – larger, in fact, than those of the Scottish Executive or Microsoft UK; and Ken and that close members of his team were part of a revolutionary clique who wanted to create a 'city state' in the capital. For good measure it also questioned the Mayor's decision to embrace the Egyptian cleric Yusuf al-Qaradawi and Hugo Chávez, the Venezuelan President; the Conservative MP Alan Duncan, a former oil trader, popped up to call the oil-for-advice deal with Venezuela 'immoral'. The *Dispatches* allegations were perhaps best summarised by one of its contributors, the Liberal Democrat MP and sometime GLA member Lynne Featherstone: 'Ken gets away with the unacceptable. That's Ken.'

Strangely enough, the *Evening Standard* now offered Ken a rare interlude from the bad publicity – as the spotlight turned away from him and onto Boris at one of their 'Influentials' debates. Michael Eboda, the former editor of the black newspaper *New Nation*, warned Boris that what he had written about 'piccaninnies' and 'watermelon smiles' would come back to haunt him. Boris apologised in public for the first time for any offence his words caused, but insisted that they had been taken out of context. 'I do feel very sad that people have been so offended by these words and I'm sorry that I've caused this offence, but if you look at the article as written they really do not bear the construction you're putting on them. I feel very strongly that this is something which is simply not in my heart. I'm absolutely 100 per cent anti-racist, I despise and loathe racism.'

The interlude did not last long. The next day, 22 January, further allegations followed about use of City Hall resources in the form of another Gilligan story in the *Standard*, claiming that Ken's 2008 campaign website was registered in the name of his adviser on climate change, Mark Watts. The registration, which included Watts's mobile phone number, was apparently made during office hours, although Watts denied that he was the site's registered owner. At a press conference on the same day, Ken confronted the allegations about GLA staff working on his campaign. Conceding that work had been done during office hours, he insisted they had nonetheless not broken GLA rules because they all worked flexible hours. 'They get paid by the taxpayer to do work and that they do. What they do in their private time, as long as they're not using City Hall resources, is really a matter for them,' he told journalists. 'This is not an office where you clock in at nine and leave at five. When staff are working sixty or seventy hours a week, taking up a large part of their weekend, if they take half an hour out of the middle of the day to see somebody on their own time, that's fine.'

But Ken's terrible week hadn't finished yet. That night he received the news that Tim Donovan from BBC London had caught Lee Jasper's deputy, Rosemary Emodi, lying about a freebie trip to Nigeria. Emodi had denied making the trip the previous November with Errol Walters, a friend of Jasper and one of those who had benefited from LDA largesse. When presented with the evidence that she had taken the plane, she immediately resigned. Ken's opponents had their first scalp.

On Thursday Ken had a date with Jim Naughtie on the Radio 4 *Today* programme and acknowledged what was pretty obvious for all to see: this had been the 'worst week' of his mayoral term. But he was in pugilistic mood – attacking his critics, defending his friends. He said that Brenda Stern, one of the ex-City Hall employees who complained about irregularities at the LDA, had been sacked after 'she was intimidatory to the staff working for her and the entire senior management team said it was impossible to work with her'. Stern later threatened to sue over the claim. By contrast Ken hugged Jasper close, telling Naughtie: 'I trust Lee with my life.' He defended himself against some of the claims in the *Dispatches* documentary, arguing that his attacks on Trevor Phillips were about Phillips's views, and 'not anti-him'. It hardly rang true, yet as the interview moved on Ken soon disarmed his host by accepting the tough premise on which much of the interview seemed to be based: when Naughtie asked whether he wasn't really operating his office like a personal fiefdom the Mayor answered simply: 'Yes.' He went on: 'That's exactly what Tony Blair – and I was opposed to the idea at the beginning – set out to create … I am accountable to Londoners; I can't blame anybody else if it's going wrong.' For an interviewer there is nothing more awkward than having your premise accepted like that: it really stuffs your interview strategy, and Ken was to use the tactic several times throughout the campaign. On the other hand it certainly guarantees making news, and his opponents weren't slow to jump on the apparent admission. 'Mayor Livingstone effectively said this morning that he is entitled to act like a dictator because the law allows him to,' Brian Paddick complained, whilst Boris said: 'Never mind the whisky, Ken Livingstone is clearly drunk on power.'

The final week of January saw some of the pressure lift from Ken, as the stream of revelations slowed. Aside from allegations that mayoral aide Kevin Austin had buried news of a TfL report which showed that allowing motorbikes to use bus lanes cut accidents, the next few days were about Boris and polls – and they contained good news for Ken. First came a YouGov poll putting him on 44 per cent, Boris on 40 per cent and Paddick on 8 per cent. Coming after the *Dispatches* allegations and Emodi's resignation, it was welcome news at Camp Ken.

Next came the revelation that Boris had accepted office space in County Hall from Shirayama Europe, a company which in the past had had disputes with Ken. Boris denied the allegations: 'This is a donation and has been registered as such. This type of story from Ken's campaign goes to show how low they are prepared to go.' But it was not Boris's last donation-related story. In the *Observer* that Sunday, the Pendennis column carried news that Labour backbencher John Mann would report Boris for failing to declare to House of Commons authorities donations totalling £234,000. On closer examination it didn't add up to much of a story – all the donations had been registered with the Electoral Commission, and the Conservatives had received advice from the Commons authorities that they didn't have to do it twice. These stories may have been trifling, but they came at a time when funding scandals were swirling around the Conservative MP Derek Conway, who had paid his sons tens of thousands of pounds as his researchers when in fact they had been at university. The media were reporting any minor infraction as a serious breach, and these stories appeared to level the sleaze playing field between the top two mayoral candidates.

The next poll also contained mixed news for both candidates. A ComRes survey of business leaders for the *Independent* showed that although they thought Boris was a 'buffoon', they still preferred him to Ken. More than half of those questioned thought Ken had been divisive and too left wing.

As a month of extraordinary turmoil in both main campaigns came to an end, there was finally time for some light relief in the form of a series of endorsements. Boris was first to benefit, as he received backing from the Beard Liberation Front, albeit in a slightly backhanded way. His famously chaotic hairstyle was an 'essential part of his character', they said, and he should not give in to his minders and discard it. Paddick was the next beneficiary – and his endorsement came from a slightly more glamorous quarter as Sir Elton John added his backing to the struggling Liberal Democrat campaign and hosted a celebrity fundraiser to help generate it some much-needed cash.

Finally, more than twenty artists – including the reclusive graffiti muralist Banksy, Antony Gormley and Jeremy Deller – would donate works of art for an auction in aid of Ken's mayoral campaign.

At the end of January the candidates faced very similar challenges to those they had faced a month earlier. Nick Cohen summed up the position in a rather despairing tirade in the *Standard*. 'My dilemma,' he wrote: 'Ken is past it and Boris hasn't a clue.' His complaint about Boris – that he was still thinking on the go and didn't seem to have the policy heft to back up the eloquence and passion – would be addressed over the next few weeks as the Conservative campaign began to churn out policies on an almost daily basis. But on 30 January, before that began, Ken had his annual budget speech to enjoy. Making full political use of it, he set out plans for 1,000 extra police officers to patrol London's streets. As so often with Ken, all was not quite as it seemed: most of the new police were funded by the Government and not by the council tax payer. Nevertheless it was a major piece of news, and it allowed Ken to face a difficult month with some new policy substance.

February: Policies ahoy!

February started much as January had – with more pressure on Ken Livingstone's senior staff. This time it was the *Times* which had obtained leaked emails and published them on 1 February. They showed that during the 2004 mayoral election Ken's former adviser on Asian affairs, Atma Singh, had been asked to write articles in support of him, and to do so during office hours. This contradicted claims Ken had made just the week before that no-one on his staff had broken the law, 'which is that they can't publicly campaign, which is they can't make a speech for me or write an article for me'. Singh also claimed that during the election 90 per cent of his time had been spent campaigning and only 10 per cent on the job. Ken's office claimed that the rules only prohibited writing articles published in that individual's name, not in Ken's name, but Boris Johnson and Brian Paddick leaped on the new revelations to call for a full investigation. Later that afternoon the *Evening Standard* reported that another organisation funded by the London Development Agency and associated with Lee Jasper had been referred to the police, bringing the total to six. At the weekend the Conservative and the Liberal Democrat campaigns threatened to refer Ken to the Electoral Commission regarding his use of the Mayor's free paper, the *Londoner*, known as 'Ken's *Pravda*' by his enemies on the London Assembly, during the campaign.

None of this, of course, was taking place in a vacuum. Whilst the

London mayoralty was the biggest prize up for grabs on 1 May it wasn't the only prize. Local elections across England and Wales would be the first electoral test for both Gordon Brown and Nick Clegg, and the first time the three men expected to lead their parties into the next general election would face each other. With three months to go before the elections, hints of skittishness began to appear in the press. First to fret was Brown: according to the *Daily Telegraph* he had begun to fear that Ken would lose the election. An appearance by Ken at the recent Davos summit had got senior Labour figures worried: 'If we lost London it would be a political disaster. And Gordon knows it,' one Cabinet source was quoted as saying. But Brown was not alone. As the chances of London actually backing Boris rose, so too did doubts about whether he could really pull off the job of being Mayor, and they surfaced in a much-discussed Philip Stephens piece in the *Financial Times*. 'I have heard one senior Tory say the best outcome would be for Ken Livingstone to win by a handful of votes,' he wrote. 'The party would have shown it is back in serious contention, whilst avoiding the risk of Mr Johnson making a hash of it.' He claimed that senior Conservatives were unsure whether surrounding Boris on all sides with technocrats would be enough to ensure that he could 'leave behind a political career built on flamboyant idiosyncrasies for the gritty task of running City Hall.'

The start of the second week, 4 February, was marked by the introduction of the LEZ, or low emissions zone. The LEZ is an attempt to cut emissions by charging hauliers and delivery companies which use older, more polluting vehicles £200 to drive into the zone. Like many Ken innovations, it is hugely controversial and its promised benefits are much in dispute. Boris called it 'the most punitive, draconian fining regime in the whole of Europe' and promised to review it. Interestingly, Paddick promised to scrap it entirely, arguing that not only would it not achieve its stated aims, it would cost millions of pounds to run and disproportionately affect small operators and families on low incomes.

This new policy-related intermission didn't last long, though, before the campaign reverted to Ken's management style and his handling of LDA money. Later that day a report into LDA grants commissioned by the London Assembly found that the agency's processes were 'seriously flawed', with little evidence that it had investigated whether the projects spent money properly or achieved the stated objectives. And the next day the *Evening Standard* carried details of another Andrew Gilligan investigation, this time showing that many of the groups which had backed Ken and attacked Boris had been generously funded by various parts of the Mayor's empire. With all this swirling around it was perhaps the perfect time for Boris to make some concrete suggestions about how to deal with it. This he did, on 5 February announcing a package of measures including the commitment that, if elected, he would serve no more than two terms in office and support legislation to require the same of his successors. 'The whole thing has become seamy and out of control,' he told LBC radio. One insider on Ken's campaign later acknowledged the power of this 'two terms' argument.

The next few days were dominated by more allegations about Jasper and the LDA. On 7 February the London Assembly finally got its teeth into the subject, questioning Ken and several of his senior advisers. One, the LDA chief executive, Manny Lewis, admitted that some of Jasper's behaviour was 'not appropriate' and sometimes 'not the way an adviser should interact with the LDA'. But it was a string of emails released to Assembly members as part of its investigation which really put the cat among the pigeons. They showed that hundreds of thousands of pounds had been allocated without proper paperwork or proper competition, and appeared to contradict claims by Jasper that he had not got involved in funding decisions. Opposition politicians piled on the pressure, Paddick saying Jasper's position was no longer tenable and he should resign. Later that day the first cracks appeared in Ken's case for the defence. He admitted that his original comment about there being a 'full audit trail' for LDA money was made off the cuff and 'wasn't true', and revealed that 'until we got the result of the audit investigation a couple of weeks ago, we didn't know. We didn't know any money wasn't accounted for.' But if cracks were appearing, that didn't mean Ken would back down. He staunchly supported Jasper and laid into his critics, accusing them of a 'racist smear campaign against Lee Jasper ... I fear this is going to be a divisive, racist campaign.' It provided an opportunity for Boris to fight back on this ground: 'This old-school, 1980s divisive style of politics shows how out of touch Ken has become. His responses to questions are ridiculous.'

On 9 February Andrew Grice used his political column in the *Independent* to make the case that the contest in London mattered for national politics, but his most interesting point was about the damage Gilligan's stories in the *Evening Standard* were doing to Ken's campaign. The Labour campaign, foreshadowing a general election pitch of Gordon Brown against David Cameron, tried to 'frame the choice as between Mr Livingstone's experience and competence and the image and inexperience of Mr Johnson'. The problem, wrote Grice, was that 'the "competence" tag is in danger of slipping' because of the stories in the *Standard*. He added, for good measure, that in addition to reaching commuters from outer London boroughs, the *Standard* was read by 'every journalist in London ... and it is influential in setting their agenda, which could be bad news for Labour as the national media turns its attention to the mayoral contest'. It was a prescient piece.

The next day Boris was again in the papers, this time criticising the siting of Heathrow as a 'planning error' and suggesting that it might be better to close it altogether and look at building a new airport on artificial islands in the Thames estuary. 'Heathrow on Sea', as the *Sunday Times* dubbed it, might cost about the same as a third runway at Heathrow.

On Sunday morning, a newly coiffed Boris, his hair verging on the neat and tidy, arrived early at BBC Television Centre in west London for his first national television interview of 2008. Appearing on *The Andrew Marr Show*, Boris had had plenty of time to work on his messages, and as he strode into the studio he was determined to get them out. What followed, though, were new messages and a new haircut but the same old Boris chaos. As Marr gently probed him, Boris simply talked... and talked. What must have been worrying for his handlers was that it didn't appear deliberate – he wasn't taking breaths mid-sentence to prevent an interruption at the end, like Margaret Thatcher used to. It was just good, old-fashioned message indiscipline: thinking on the hoof. Still he did – eventually – manage to get out his news, announcing his 'Payback London' plan – giving teenagers who had had their free bus travel removed the chance to earn it back through community service. 'I think it would be a good way of connecting people with the privilege they're getting and making them value it,' he said. After that appearance barely a day would pass until polling day when one of the candidates didn't pop up on some media outlet for an interview. For the party activists and journalists who followed events day in, day out, it could become very dreary at times, but in truth none of the candidates could go for long without saying something interesting or controversial, and this kept the campaign exciting.

Still, constant interviews didn't remove the need to keep making the news, and the next week Ken used his mayoral prerogative to make major transport announcements on Monday 11 and Tuesday

12 February. Cycling was first: a £500 million, ten-year plan to effect a 'cycling and walking transformation of London'. The plan included commuter cycling routes and a central London bike hire scheme along the lines of the Velib' scheme in Paris, as well as Bike Zones for shoppers and improvements both in central and outer London to make walking easier. Ken predicted that the scheme would save 1.6 million tons of carbon dioxide per year, although it emerged shortly afterwards that he hadn't properly consulted the London boroughs in advance about the commuter cycle routes – crucial since many of the routes are on roads for which the boroughs have responsibility. It was also a move into opposition territory since Boris was one of the best-known bicyclists in Britain. Having apparently first considered running for Mayor whilst on his bicycle and trying to overtake a bendy bus, he had looked set to make the policy area his own. The next day brought confirmation of a new scheme to tackle the most polluting vehicles – increasing the congestion charge to a whopping £25 for band G cars. 'Nobody needs to damage the environment by driving a gas-guzzling Chelsea tractor in central London,' declared the Mayor, but whilst this band included limousines and sports cars, it also included some family cars which were much more modest. Crucially, those living in the zone and paying the new higher charge would not be eligible for the 90 per cent discount normally available. They would be hit with a bill for up to £6,500 a year. At the same time a long list of small cars with the lowest emissions (those in bands A and B) would be able to enter the congestion zone free. Ken's critics jumped on the proposals, with Boris denouncing them as an 'old-style, tax-the-motorist' policy. More surprisingly Paddick, the supposedly green Liberal Democrat, joined him in opposing the measure, arguing that whilst families would be hit, 'rich people with gas guzzlers will continue to pay the congestion charge even at £25'. Critics also complained that allowing thousands of extra small cars

into the zone would increase congestion, the primary target of the scheme.

On Wednesday the focus shifted away from Ken, as Boris launched his first major set of policies: his crime manifesto. He did so with the Shadow Home Secretary, David Davis, at his side and with that a moral pat on the shoulder from the national party, an implicit rebuttal to all the talk that they didn't really want him to win. The principle underlying his attack on crime would, Boris said, be that 'by systematically tackling small crimes we can drive out more serious criminality. I believe that we can change the lives of kids who would otherwise be sucked into a nightmarish culture of violence and crimi-nality.' And in a pattern which would be seen throughout his many policy announcements over the next couple of months the emphasis would be on small, concrete steps. He would follow Paddick's lead and chair the Metropolitan Police Authority; he would scrap some press officers and hire more police officers (a good line); he would try live CCTV on buses; he would hire more safer transport teams for the buses and give more powers to ticket inspectors; he would fund more rape crisis centres; he would increase police accountability by holding regular monthly meetings and introducing New York-style crime mapping. Above all, he said, he would better fund and more closely work with the voluntary sector to give children alternatives to crime, and when he sat down he received the warm endorsement of Ray Lewis from the Eastside Young Leaders Academy. In addition to being based on small steps, much of this was very traditional Conservative fare. He never sounded more so than when he railed against 'the gen-eral increase in incivility', but was happy to do so. 'That may be the type of thing you expect from a Conservative,' he told his audience at the end, 'but I am a Conservative.' For a party which only months before was still in the middle of having its brand decontaminated, this was heady stuff. His audience clapped him out.

His rivals were not applauding. Paddick in particular, who had hoped to make crime the centrepiece of his appeal to voters, laid into Boris for being 'clueless', saying Payback London would be 'unenforceable and unrealistic' and that publishing crime statistics would 'further isolate the most disadvantaged in London, who already suffer disproportionate levels of crime'. 'Boris Johnson's crime policies will do for London what he did for the people of Portsmouth and Liverpool: unfairly label decent law-abiding people as hooligans and criminals,' he claimed. Paddick had his own plans for dealing with disorder on public transport, which he announced the next day as part of his transport manifesto. It included women-friendly Tube carriages with guards on duty and, in a pretty shameless play to the outer boroughs, levying a £10 Greater London congestion charge with only Londoners and delivery vehicles exempted.

Meanwhile on the same day that Boris had been railing against general incivility, Ken was doing his own bit to add to it. Appearing in front of the London Assembly to answer questions about the scandal over LDA grants, he accused its members of being 'sanctimonious hypocrites' for attacking Lee Jasper whilst delaying summoning him to answer questions. The meeting had to be adjourned until he calmed down. This was not an isolated incident: Ken had become increasingly contemptuous of some London Assembly members over the last few years. His supporters argued that the many occasions on which he was needled and abused by Assembly members never made the headlines whilst the relatively few occasions on which he snapped always did, but that is the nature of the Mayor's rather more exalted role, and as one of the country's most media-savvy politicians he would have known it.

Earlier that day the four main candidates had made their way to the first hustings of the campaign, hosted by the Green Alliance. It was an entertaining but sometimes testy affair as the candidates sought both to burnish their green credentials and to get in a crack at the opposition. Boris made plenty of jokes, offering to give Ken free cycling lessons: 'It is high time that, like me and every other cyclist in London, you face the full horror of trying to overtake a bendy bus.' But he made plenty of sharp political jabs, too: as the *Independent* reported the next day, it was 'Serious Boris rather than Buffoon Boris' on show. Ken had some points of his own to make. 'You can't have candidates saying … that "I am going to be the greenest Mayor ever but I applauded George Bush for not signing the Kyoto treaty". It is rubbish,' he said. Siân Berry was well received by a sympathetic audience and Paddick argued that he had the smallest carbon footprint of all four. He had had the heating on in his one-bedroom flat for only forty-five minutes during the winter, he revealed.

The next day, Friday, it was back to business as usual with a very uncontrite Ken talking about Jasper. This time, though, the record had changed: finally bowing to the inevitable he had suspended his aide. But Ken did not leave it at that, as he called in the police to investigate the charges – his critics should 'put up or shut up' – and allow Jasper to clear his name. In typically intemperate language he said he expected Jasper would be exonerated and 'show this to be a shameful campaign'. An enormous Andrew Gilligan piece in the *Evening Standard* reminded its readers of the six police investigations already under way, just how many of the suspicious LDA-funded organisations had been run by friends of Jasper, and how big a problem this still represented for the Mayor. As the *Times* noted the following day, it was 'brutal political calculation' which had moved the Mayor, who just three weeks before had declared he would trust Jasper with his life, to suspend him. Jasper's response a couple of days later was as robust as Ken's had been brutal. 'I am not guilty of anything so that is why I asked the police to investigate. To simply resign and have no police investigation, I would not be able to completely prove my innocence,' he told the black community newspaper the *Voice*. 'I am not being hounded out of my job because of racist lies and smears. I am not capitulating to racism. I never do.' He strongly denied that he had inappropriately used his influence with the LDA projects. Jasper said he would be spending his time whilst suspended (although still on his full £120,000 salary) working with Operation Black Vote to get black Londoners to the polling stations. All laudable enough, except that he also said Ken was the 'candidate of choice' in the election. The endorsement appeared to be a clear breach of the rules, and Nick Cohen launched a scathing attack on Jasper for hijacking Operation Black Vote and turning it into a vehicle for Ken. 'Everything about its turn into party politics is wrong,' he wrote. 'Rival parties see that the pressure group they helped in good faith is now a "Re-elect Ken" campaign, while taxpayers are forced yet again to wonder why their money is going astray.'

The next news for Ken and his suspended aide was rather better, although it still left them in a fix. Just days after Ken had announced it, on Wednesday 20 February Scotland Yard revealed that it was not investigating Jasper after all. 'To date, there have been no criminal allegations reported to us in connection with this individual,' said a statement from the Met, revealing that although Ken had referred the matter to the police, it appeared that the alleged misconduct was just that – misconduct – and not criminality. On the surface this was excellent news, and the *Guardian* certainly responded with a positive headline, 'Mayor's aide cleared of fraud'. But Ken's critics on the London Assembly were furious, believing that Ken had known all along there were no allegations of criminality on Jasper's part, and that the suspension had been a ruse to remove Jasper for the duration of the election. Ken would eventually ask the Met to look again at the allegations.

Although there seemed little Ken's critics could do about the

Mayor, they still had a powerful ally in the form of the battering ram that was the *Evening Standard*. And on the same day as Jasper was defending himself in the *Voice*, it launched a new assault on the Mayor's position, this time over the apparently arcane subject of pollsters. This story saw two threads coming together. The first was long-standing concern over the use Ken made of polls carried out for his office by Ipsos MORI: he revealed only the parts of polls which favoured his position. According to British Polling Council (BPC) rules, Ipsos MORI should, when its client had revealed part of the survey, have posted the full details of the questions on its website within two days. Ipsos MORI claimed there was a conflict in the rules between the BPC and the Market Research Society (MRS) and that in such a situation they would abide by the MRS rules. But not all observers were convinced this was the real reason. One, quoted in the *Standard*, wondered whether other questions had been asked in the survey which shouldn't have been, as part of a publicly funded poll. There was a second thread to this story, though, and that was the running battle between YouGov, which runs internet-based polls for the *Standard* and the *Daily Telegraph*, and many other pollsters, who regard internet polls as unproven. Crucially, the Mayor was in this latter camp, and this story in the *Standard* did look like an attempt to provide some cover for YouGov when its methodology was under attack from the Mayor.

The next day, 19 February, saw *Time Out*'s editor-at-large, Michael Hodges, launch his bid for the Mayor's office, whilst the German car manufacturer Porsche launched a legal challenge over the proposed £25 congestion charge. Calling it 'unfair and disproportionate', Porsche had a big stake in the outcome: almost every one of its models would fall into the higher category. Amazingly, both Boris and Brian Paddick said they could understand where Porsche was coming from, even if they didn't go so far as to back the legal action.

In the meantime Boris was given a rap over the knuckles for not registering speedily enough a £25,000 donation from the Conservative peer Lord Laidlaw. Ken gave an interview to the *Guardian* in which he appeared far more relaxed and happy than he sometimes had in public. 'I love it. I love the fight. I love winning, and even when I'm losing I still love the job,' he told Helene Mulholland. 'Whatever my personality skill set says, it's perfect for this.' On Sunday 24th it was Ken's turn to appear on *The Andrew Marr Show*, where he was quizzed about the latest state of play on Lee Jasper. Ken didn't miss a beat, laying into the *Evening Standard* for claiming it had only ever accused Jasper of misconduct and nothing criminal. 'Well,' said Ken, 'misconduct is a criminal offence in public office, it actually carries life, a maximum prison sentence of life imprisonment, so it's very serious.' And he revealed that if nothing was proved, Jasper would be reinstated. There was a typical Ken flourish when he was asked about the £25 congestion charge. Would he like to see these 'Chelsea tractors' priced off the road, asked Marr. 'Oh, absolutely,' he replied. It would send a message to the car manufacturers that they had to design more fuel-efficient cars.

The following morning the Mayor received strong – if predictable – support from a coalition of centre-left big cheeses. Writing a letter to the *Guardian* they called Ken 'a standard bearer for real progressive politics'. And the group, which included the paper's columnist Polly Toynbee, Tony Benn, the musician Billy Bragg, some prominent Labour MPs and the head of the Fabian Society think tank, wrote that 'Livingstone represents a hope that something better is possible; that a different type of society is not just some pipedream of the left, but can be created. This is the reason he is under such severe attack.'

Whilst Ken was receiving plaudits from the intelligentsia, Boris took a rawer political approach, catching a morning rush-hour train from Crayford to Charing Cross, hoping to appeal to commuters from the outer boroughs. Announcing his 'London Orb' plan for linking suburban town centres with express buses which would only stop at key locations or transport interchanges, he said: 'London suffers from unacceptable levels of overcrowding.' He promised to instigate a trial if elected in May, with fares held at the same level as standard buses.

That evening Ken would get the chance to mix the philosophy with raw politics at the *Evening Standard* debate. And it allowed him to bring the debate back onto his own turf: how to run a great city. He emphasised the importance of Crossrail and the need to have a competent Mayor to push it through. London could be bankrupted if it was mishandled, he warned his audience, as he received plaudits from Lionel Barber, the editor of the *Financial Times*, for his strong support for the city, and a nasty pop on the nose from LBC's Nick Ferrari for the proposed £25 congestion charge. 'Red Ken has gone green – that is, green with envy, because he doesn't like people who are doing well,' he said. Ken conceded that the direct environmental benefits of the higher charge would be limited, but perhaps the real reasons behind it had already been revealed to Andrew Marr on Sunday.

Before the month drew to a close there was just time enough for one more Jasper story. This time it was his failure to declare his chairmanship of Equanomics UK, an organisation which received £15,000 from the London Assembly. Although there was some confusion about his exact relationship with Equanomics, it all added to the sense of murkiness around his role.

Then came more polls. There were two: one a public poll for ITV's *London Tonight*, which gave Boris a 5-point lead – on 44 per cent compared to Ken on 39 per cent and Paddick on 12 per cent. The other was a private Ipsos MORI poll for the Labour Party, reported in the *Guardian*. It reported a very much more pro-Ken electorate, with him on 37 per cent, Boris on 28 per cent and Paddick on 14 per cent. In a straight run-off election Ken would win by 49 per cent to Boris's 47 per cent among those certain to vote. This disparity between the pollsters would continue throughout the campaign, with YouGov's online polls consistently showing a bigger lead for Boris and the other polls, conducted using more traditional telephone techniques, finding more Ken voters.

On 27 February, Boris made a claim which would be tested repeatedly over the next few months, and picked over in forensic detail by Ken. Speaking on BBC London radio he said the cost of employing the conductors to work on his proposed fleet of new Routemaster buses would cost just £8 million a year. It quickly became clear that because more Routemasters would be required than the bendy buses they replaced, the bill would be substantially higher than that, yet Boris would stick resolutely to his initial figure for some weeks.

The next few days again provided lighter fare to end the month. Paddick went first, answering a question from the free evening paper *London Lite* about whether he was 'out and proud or in the closet' with incredulity: 'Oh come along! My skeletons and I have been out of the closet for some time now.' He told the paper he was on Facebook rather than MySpace because 'I've been told by my advisers it's the best one to be on'. The next day it was Labour's deputy leader, Harriet Harman, providing a semi-comic interlude. 'Whatever you do, don't vote for the appalling Boris Johnson,' she apparently told a Labour for Turkey event in Parliament. 'Would that be the Boris Johnson who is the grandson of a Turkish refugee, descended from a famous Turkish politician and related to a former Turkish Ambassador to London?' wondered Hugo Rifkind in the *Times*. Finally it was Boris's turn, although his comic interlude provided the opportunity both for the *Daily Telegraph* to run a funny picture, and for Boris to make a serious political point. It followed news that he was being investigated by the Met – for purloining the cigar case of Tariq Aziz, the former Iraqi Deputy Prime Minister, five years earlier. Boris had written about lifting the case in the *Telegraph* at the time, but now Scotland Yard, after being alerted to the incident, sent him a letter asking about 'Iraqi cultural property'. During an election campaign in which crime had loomed large it was a gift, and Boris accepted it eagerly. He was said to be 'fuming': 'There were over 18,000 crimes in London last month and yet the police write to me about this,' he said, incredulously.

1–15 March: General Jasper

March began with Labour activists attending the party's spring conference over a weekend in Birmingham. Boris-bashing seemed to be the order of the day, with Ken Livingstone leading from the front when he described his opponent as 'George W. Boris', claiming that he had done 'more U-turns than a London black cab' regarding his position on the Kyoto treaty on climate change. Hazel Blears, the Communities and Local Government Secretary, was among others to join the offensive, branding him 'a nasty right-wing elitist, with odious views and criminal friends like Conrad Black'.

If nothing else, it demonstrated that senior Labour figures were viewing him as a serious threat, although Boris Johnson himself expressed disappointment with the way the campaign was being waged against him. 'I have been subject to some of the most personal attacks we have seen in politics in recent years and I have also been repeatedly accused of proposing cuts in vital services – all made by senior Labour politicians who are desperate to cover up that their candidate has a lack of new ideas,' he lamented.

That Sunday, Brian Paddick appeared on *The Andrew Marr Show* on BBC One, where he launched a dual attack on Ken and the Metropolitan Police Commissioner, Sir Ian Blair, asserting that 'there does seem to be a bit of collusion going on between the two'. He also attacked Ken for having chosen not to chair the

Metropolitan Police Authority, given that tackling crime was the biggest issue for Londoners. On that issue, he pleaded: 'Surely you should have the expert on crime as Mayor if that is your number one concern?'

The following day was an important one for Boris: the launch of his transport manifesto at a hall near St Pancras station. Among the many pledges he made were: doubling the number of police officers patrolling buses and funding extra police officers to patrol stations, phasing out bendy buses and running a competition to design a new Routemaster, protecting the Freedom Pass, introducing 'Payback London', ensuring all Tube stations always have a manned ticket office, running the Tube later on Friday and Saturday night, looking to negotiate a no-strike deal with the Tube unions, stopping the introduction of the £25 congestion charge for the most polluting cars whilst allowing people to pay the existing charge by direct debit, introducing a bike hire scheme, allowing motorcycles to use bus lanes, and opposing a third runway at Heathrow. 'We hear nothing but the same old out-of-date solutions from a Labour Mayor who has run out of ideas,' he said.

Ken derided Boris's plans as 'chaotic' and 'vacuous'. His campaign said that Boris's policy on buses would mean a 15 per cent increase in fares, a claim which would be repeated by the Transport Secretary, Ruth Kelly, in the Commons the following day. But she got rebuked by the Speaker, Michael Martin, when she said that Boris was 'more suited to a role in the circus'. Also on the transport front, Boris condemned as 'a ludicrous waste of taxpayers' money' the news that Ken was sending a London double-decker bus and eight drivers to the Olympics in Beijing at a cost of £450,000.

Paddick, meanwhile, claimed to have received a 'major boost' with the defection of Dirk Hazell, a former chairman of the London Conservatives, saying it had 'added further momentum to his campaign'.

This was not especially convincing, not least because no-one outside the innermost Tory circles had ever heard of him.

Tuesday 4 March was to prove a landmark in the campaign, with the scalp of Lee Jasper being claimed by the end of the day. And, no surprise, it was an Andrew Gilligan story which prompted his resignation. The revelation on the front page of the *Evening Standard* was that £100,000 of public money had been given to projects run by a woman, Karen Chouhan, to whom Jasper had written a number of sexually charged emails, leaked to the *Standard*, of course.

'Happy birthday my gorgeous, wonderful, sexy Kazzi … Darling … I want to wisk [*sic*] you away to a deserted island beach, honey-glase [*sic*] you, let you cook slowly before a torrid and passionate embrace,' read one of the messages sent from Jasper's City Hall email account to Chouhan, company secretary of the 1990 Trust and director of the Black Londoners' Forum (BLF) until November 2007. Another email he sent declared: 'I love thee [*sic*] feet, ankles, legs, thighs, bum and belly, arms, head and brain. But most of all I love you in a flaming red sari, bangles, chains or failing that in a bikini!' He signed his email: 'Your man, General Jasper.'

Jasper had not declared a relationship of any kind with Chouhan, although she denied there had ever been a sexual relationship between them. 'There is a close relationship, that's for sure, but there's never been an affair,' she said. 'I am a happily married woman.' She added that his messages were 'just banter' and denied any suggestion of impropriety over the money paid to the BLF or the 1990 Trust. Jasper said he wouldn't comment on matters relating to his private life, but announced that he was resigning from his role at City Hall. 'It has become clear that a number of matters which are not of first importance in London are being used to distract from the crucial questions in the election campaign,' he wrote in his resignation letter. 'The racist nature of a relentless media campaign and the consequent effects on myself and family have placed an intolerable strain on all of us. I have decided to put a stop to this by tendering my resignation.'

In a separate development, a BBC London investigation had discovered that Jasper had failed to register all the free travel and accommodation he enjoyed during a trip to the United States and the Caribbean in 2006.

At a meeting in Richmond that night, Ken echoed Jasper's sentiments about the media and gave him his fullest backing. 'I think it has been an absolutely disgraceful campaign,' he stated. 'It will be months before the police finish their inquiries. But I would bet my own life that they will clear Lee Jasper and I will reappoint him when they do.' But Ken's opponents could not agree less. Boris said that it was 'further proof that Ken Livingstone has had his day', whilst Paddick said that Jasper's resignation 'raises serious questions about the Mayor's judgement and his improbable claims that there is nothing wrong with his administration'.

There was also frustration from Ken's opponents at the timing of Jasper's departure, since he (Jasper) had been due to appear before the London Assembly for the first time at ten o'clock the following morning. He was due to answer questions about his role in the funding of what were by that stage understood to be at least fourteen organisations run by friends of his, to the tune of £3.8 million, as uncovered during the previous three months by the *Evening Standard*.

The following day the repercussions were felt, with John Ross, Ken's economics adviser, admitting that Jasper had breached City Hall rules by failing to declare his position on the board of Equanomics UK, a body which was 'incubated' by the 1990 Trust. Ross was appearing at the Assembly session which Jasper would otherwise have attended and seemed to break ranks with Ken by criticising Jasper's many outside interests. 'I don't believe that people who have positions [in the GLA] should have interests in regard to them,' he said. 'I think they should declare all matters. My actual personal view is that directors of the GLA should not be holding directorships, companies and so on.'

Meanwhile, along the river at Westminster, David Cameron raised the matter at Prime Minister's Questions in the Commons, but Gordon Brown sidestepped the questions. The exchange went as follows:

> *David Cameron*: There are currently six police investigations under way into the conduct of government in London. The most recent allegations are that the London Mayor's director for equalities and policing has been channelling public funds into organisations run by friends and cronies. Does the Prime Minister agree with me that that is completely unacceptable?

> *Gordon Brown*: As on any occasion when a matter referring to a police investigation is raised, I have to say this is a matter for the police. It should be fully investigated, but it is not a matter for this House until the police complete their investigations.

> *DC*: The point is that while these accusations are going on and this investigation is under way, the Mayor – the Labour Mayor – has said that he trusts Lee Jasper with his life and last night he said that he is already planning to reappoint him. Does not every element of the Prime Minister's moral compass tell him that this is wrong?

> *GB*: As I understand it, the person whom the right hon. Gentleman is talking about has resigned and is no longer in that employment.

It was not the last time Ken's record was discussed in the Commons, and observers noted that on each occasion the Prime Minister studiously avoided referring to Ken by name, instead stiffly talking about 'the Labour Mayor' or 'the Mayor of London'. Lee Jasper was to be the only story in town for the best part of forty-eight hours, with Boris seizing on Ken's woes the following day when he relaunched and expanded his plans to make City Hall and the Mayor's staff more open, transparent and accountable. He said that if elected, he would publish the biographies, responsibilities and contact details of all mayoral advisers on the City Hall website for the public to see; he would introduce a code of conduct similar to the rules for ministerial special advisers; a register of interests covering all staff at the Greater London Authority, including the Mayor's office, would be published online and updated regularly; and mayoral advisers would be held to account regularly at question-and-answer sessions with the London Assembly.

Ken, meanwhile, followed Ross's admission of the previous day by saying Jasper had indeed breached the rules and he was 'disappointed' about that, but reiterated his defence of his long-standing friend on LBC radio. 'He sent some silly emails, no-one disagrees with that, it's very embarrassing,' he said. 'It's clearly not appropriate but that doesn't mean to say that Lee Jasper has had any financial benefit from anything that he's done as my race adviser. Before all these emails came out we were dealing with very serious allegations of fraud … He resigned because this stuff is embarrassing. It's not illegal, it's embarrassing.' Ken and his team continued to reject as a complete travesty the notion that there was corruption at City Hall, since no-one had benefited financially from any of the grants in question. But the relentless drumbeat of negative headlines made it hard for the campaign to get on the front foot.

By Thursday night, Ken was all smiles again, as his campaign hosted an auction at Farringdon's Aquarium Gallery to raise funds for his re-election bid. Banksy's *Sketch for Essex Road* fetched an impressive £195,000 from a mystery bidder, although the individual's identity would have to emerge when the Labour Party declared its donations to the Electoral Commission. Millionaire Labour MP Geoffrey Robinson parted with £5,000 for a work by Jo Wonder, whilst Ken's Deputy Mayor, Nicky Gavron, was rumoured to have bought a sketch by Antony Gormley for £6,800. Ken couldn't let the evening pass without making a political point, of course. 'I suppose the artists are aware of what is happening. They recognise that if Boris gets in there will be barbarism, so they're doing everything they can to help,' he told a reporter.

The following day, at the end of a dramatic week, Transport Minister and London MP Jim Fitzpatrick weighed in behind the claims made by Ken's campaign earlier in the week that Boris's sums on his bus policies didn't add up. Ken's camp insisted that replacing bendy buses with Routemasters, complete with conductors, would cost £112 million a year and not £8 million, but a spokesman for Boris stood by his figures, pointing out: 'They are comparing the capacity of an old Routemaster, we are commissioning a new one.'

Most of the candidates kept a relatively low media profile that weekend. Brian Paddick was attending the Liberal Democrats' spring conference in Liverpool and Boris popped up briefly for an interview on Sky News with Adam Boulton, but he also found time to speak at a crime summit organised by the Conservative-controlled Hammersmith & Fulham Council and to visit Camden Market, site of a fire in February. Ken left John Ross to make a rare television appearance on the Sunday lunchtime, on the London edition of BBC One's *Politics Show* with the BBC's London political editor, Tim Donovan. Ross grew increasingly incensed at Donovan's line of questioning about the Lee Jasper affair, exclaiming: 'You said you were going to let me talk about other things, let me deal with the general context. You are attempting to divert the interest of London away from the most important matters.'

Monday 10 March saw Ken become the last of the three main candidates to launch a transport manifesto. 'I am running on my record of successfully delivering major improvements in London's transport system in the last eight years and on delivering the even bigger schemes to come,' he declared in Stratford, highlighting the Crossrail scheme and the Tube modernisation as large projects which he said he could be trusted to deliver on time and on budget. He again attacked Boris's bus costings, claiming that they emphasised the risk of transport and financial disasters if his rival was elected to run London. Ken's pledges included: introducing a new fleet of hybrid-powered buses; bringing in the £25 congestion charge for so-called 'gas-guzzling' cars; making the Freedom Pass valid twenty-four hours a day; introducing new minute-by-minute bus information technology; introducing a bike hire scheme in central London; and introducing a 'hassle-free' system for paying the congestion charge.

Boris responded by attacking him on two counts: firstly, he asserted that Ken's record of delivery was not as successful as he had claimed, with major projects having fallen behind schedule and 'gone way over budget'; secondly, he accused him of stealing his policies, for example the announcement of free travel for injured veterans, which Boris had also included in his transport manifesto and actually first mooted in a *Spectator* article in 2007.

Paddick, for his part, accused his rivals of 'bickering' and 'petty squabbling', principally over the row about the cost of Boris's policies, and insisted that the solution to London's transport crisis was to bring back trams. The Liberal Democrat candidate also announced his newest campaign team member: Rick Ridder, an American political strategist who had worked previously for the Liberal Democrats and more recently spent time on Howard Dean's (unsuccessful) bid for the 2004 Democratic presidential nomination and on Hillary Clinton's increasingly beleaguered bid for the same nomination for 2008. Paddick would later reveal that Ridder had cost 'about $50,000' and was principally paid for by Sir Elton John.

Boris again turned his fire not only on Ken but also on the Government, as he made a speech at Bloomberg and wrote an article for the *Evening Standard* about the cost of living in London. Citing London as the 'motor of the British economy', he said: 'With only 12 per cent of the population, we account for 19 per cent of GDP – and that means we make a massive net contribution to the Exchequer of £17.8 billion. And what do we get in exchange, from this Scottish Chancellor and his Scottish Prime Minister? I will tell you what we get. We get ripped off.' He said that it was a 'real disgrace' that Ken was not standing up for Londoners to demand that the capital got its fair share, and he attacked the Mayor's role in making life more expensive through increases in Tube fares and the GLA precept on the council tax – as well as some of his more profligate spending on 'vainglorious foreign policy ventures' and the *Londoner*, which Boris memorably described as 'the Mayor's ludicrous Pyongyang-style newspaper'.

Transport and crime again figured highly on the campaign trail the next day. Ken renewed his attack on Boris's bus policy. It was beginning to feel as if it was the only weak spot Ken had found in his opponent's armour and he was going to concentrate his efforts on drawing attention to it. This time he compared Boris's transport manifesto to the situation of the *Titanic* after it hit the iceberg: 'It's certain the ship is going to sink and the only question that remains is whether it will take one hour or two and how many will go down with it,' he said.

Boris countered with his own attack on Ken after the *Times* that morning reported that the incumbent Mayor was 'secretly planning much wider use of congestion charging across London if he is re-elected'. The paper's transport correspondent, Ben Webster, cited a source close to Ken as having backed up his story that 'Transport for London was developing plans to introduce charging to other congested parts of the capital but was under strict orders not to disclose anything before polling day'. This enabled the Boris campaign to swiftly put out an attack leaflet to areas the paper's report said were under consideration for congestion charging, which were Harrow, Hounslow, Kingston, Sutton, Croydon, Bromley, Ilford, Romford and Wood Green. Boris's Australian strategist, Lynton Crosby, was clearly proving his worth and Ken was feeling it. 'For the first time in my life I can actually see the benefits of a rigorous deportation policy,' Ken was quoted as saying.

But speaking to the London Assembly, Peter Hendy, the Transport Commissioner, denied outright the suggestions in the *Times* report. 'The Mayor has no plans whatever to extend the congestion charge zone, and I do not have anybody working on all those places … The Mayor has made it clear that he would only want us to work and go forward in areas where the local authority was interested … We have not been asked to do any work in any of those places.'

That morning, the three main mayoral candidates all trooped off to the House of Commons to appear before the Home Affairs Select Committee. Ken, true to form, was the most controversial, returning to an earlier theme in which he effectively blamed Margaret Thatcher for the levels of crime and anti-social behaviour. 'Looking at the generation today, these are children of the kids that grew up in the 1980s, when everyone was talking about getting your snouts in the trough, "there's no such thing as society", "greed is good",' he said. Boris hit back, suggesting that Ken would blame 'anyone but himself or his

Government for the failure to protect our teenagers against violence in London'.

During the visit to Westminster, Paddick also popped along to Downing Street to deliver a petition containing 50,000 signatures protesting against the closure of post offices across London. On seeing him pictured outside No. 10, it was hard not to conclude that this was the nearest that Paddick would get to political power during the course of the campaign.

Ken, ever delighted to be endorsed by celebrities, was joined by Kevin Spacey, the director of the Old Vic theatre, to highlight a new pot of London Development Agency money being made available to allow smaller arts bodies to bid for cash in advance of the 2012 Olympics. But not everyone from the arts world was giving Ken their full support. Tracey Emin and Dinos Chapman were among the signatories to an open letter attacking the GLA's 'relentless support for tall buildings' in east London, which, they said, 'is destroying what makes London special'. Paddick also weighed in on this issue, promising to restore 'full protection to all of London's historic views, which Ken has eroded to the benefit of his property developer friends'.

The *Evening Standard* that afternoon reported news of a first arrest in the police investigation into the funding scandal which had led to Lee Jasper's resignation. The man in question was Greg Nowell, described as 'a key associate' of Jasper, who had run the Green Badge Taxi School in Clapham – a project said to be offering training for ethnic minority taxi drivers. The investigation into that organisation had come about after Kate Hoey, the Labour MP for Vauxhall, had written in December to Sir Ian Blair, expressing her serious concerns about it.

The following day, a second arrest was reported in the *Standard*, said to be of Clive Grey, Nowell's business partner. But most political eyes were on the Commons, as the Chancellor of the Exchequer,

Alistair Darling, delivered his first Budget – which Boris said would leave Londoners worse off over the coming years. He also claimed that a reclassification of UK-registered cars included in the Budget would mean more people having to pay the £25 congestion charge for the most polluting cars if Ken were re-elected – but Ken insisted that this was not the case and that it would still only apply to cars emitting more than 225 grammes of carbon dioxide per kilometre under the new banding.

At Prime Minister's Questions immediately before the Budget statement, Gordon Brown became the latest to join the Labour attack on Boris's bus policy, claiming that fares would rise and people would be discouraged from using buses if Boris were elected Mayor. Ken, meanwhile, faced the London Assembly for the final Mayor's Question Time of his second term in office. Did he realise himself that it would be his last appearance as Mayor at such a gathering? He certainly didn't seem to show it if he did. 'I will see you all again after the great cleansing,' was his valedictory message. 'Not all of you – we are working on that.'

But what if Ken did lose? There was good news for him on this front in the Budget, as the revelation emerged, buried in the small print, that the first £30,000 of the GLA's severance pay scheme would now be tax exempt. A somewhat unusual poll also emerged which was anything but a confidence boost for Ken. Classified ads website Craigslist asked YouGov to discover from which candidate the public would least like to buy a secondhand car. Ken topped the poll at 42 per cent, with Boris on 24 per cent and Paddick scoring 5 per cent. Siân Berry scored 2 per cent – despite the fact that the committed environmentalist wouldn't have a car to sell in the first place.

At the end of the week, Ken highlighted – and claimed credit for – a 40 per cent reduction in the number of people killed or injured on London's roads during his time in office as he met road safety campaigners in north London. But he said that this was still not good enough and set a target of a 50 per cent reduction in all casualties by 2010. He also indicated a desire to work with London boroughs to increase the number of residential streets designated as 20mph zones as a further precaution to reduce road deaths.

Boris briefly left London to zip up to Gateshead for the Conservative Party's spring forum. He rallied party activists from up and down the country, encouraging them to help his campaign, by suggesting that winning the London mayoralty would give the party momentum in the run-up to the next general election. 'I want to win this election and demonstrate how different life can be under a modern Conservative Government,' he declared.

Not all were convinced by his chances, though. Talking to Andrew Pierce on LBC radio the previous weekend, one-time Conservative mayoral hopeful Lord Archer had predicted that Boris would fail in his bid to beat Ken. 'What you have to accept is you're up against one of the great political operators of all time,' he said. 'Our Ken is no fool. You'd better be awake very early in the morning and working very late at night if you're going to beat him … I think it will be very close, but as long as nothing surprising comes up from either side, I would think Ken will win it by a whisker.' He was doubtless unaware that Lynton Crosby was working up to eighteen hours a day on this job…

16–31 March: Under starter's orders

The *Sunday Times* on 16 March did not make happy reading for Ken Livingstone and Labour. Under the headline 'Support for Labour hits 25-year low' came news of a national YouGov opinion poll which showed the Conservatives opening up a 16-point lead over Labour, leading by 43 per cent to 27, with the Liberal Democrats trailing on 16 per cent. It was the largest Tory lead in such a poll since 1987 and Labour's worst rating since the party's lowest ebb under Michael Foot in 1983. Worse for Labour was the finding that in London, they were trailing by 24 per cent: even with Ken's ability to appeal to a wider support base than Labour's core vote, he would surely struggle to avoid defeat. The report predicted 'meltdown' for Labour at the 1 May elections.

Then there was the revelation in the paper that Ken's campaign for re-election in 2004 had accepted a donation from the property developer Gerald Ronson, which proved controversial for several reasons. Firstly, Ronson had been fined £5 million and spent six months in jail for his role in the Guinness share-dealing scandal; secondly, questions about cash for favours could be raised since Ken had supported Ronson's plans for Heron Tower, a 46-storey, 663-foot skyscraper in the City of London; and thirdly, it looked as though there had been a deliberate ploy to keep the donation secret, since Ronson's cheque was written for out £4,990 – exactly £10 below the threshold

at which the party would have been legally obliged to publicly identify the donor.

Ken's spokesman refused to say if any other donations had been
handled in this way and all a Labour spokesman would say was that
donations were handled 'in accordance with the rules'. Ken would
also insist whenever questions were raised about who was funding his
campaign that he never knew and didn't want to know, specifically
because he didn't want to be accused of being unduly influenced over
decisions he made.

Unconvinced by that defence, Greg Hands, the Conservative MP
for Hammersmith & Fulham, promptly lodged a complaint with the
Electoral Commission over the way in which Ken's donations were
being handled. Rather than declaring donations to himself as a 'regulated donee' under political funding laws – as Boris Johnson was
doing – Ken claimed that all gifts were raised by the Labour Party
centrally and so were declared as such. This meant that only donations of more than £5,000 to his campaign would have to be declared
(rather than the limit of £1,000 for individuals) and that they would
not have to be published until after the election, whereas the regulated
donees had to register them on a monthly basis. The Commission
announced later in the week that it had launched a review into the
allegations.

Boris, meanwhile, took time out from campaigning to run the
Sport Relief mile along Victoria Embankment, which he managed in
a creditable time of eight minutes, given the dreadful weather that
day. He had courted controversy the previous day, however, in an
interview with the *Times* in which he talked about his children being
educated in the private sector. 'His four children started at their local
state primary but when secondary loomed, "because we live in
Islington, I extracted them". Only one remains there,' stated the
write-up in the paper. Ken's campaign seized on this as 'an insult'

which was 'disdainful to every parent and teacher in the London Borough of Islington'.

The following day's *Independent* brought a minor boost for Ken: an endorsement from the former BBC director general Greg Dyke. This was ironic, since – as detailed earlier in the book – he had been touted as a possible joint candidate for the Conservatives and Liberal Democrats. 'I shall vote for Ken,' said Dyke. 'I think he's done not a bad job at all, if you look at London today compared to a decade ago it's a pretty vibrant exciting place and I think he's responsible for some of that.' It was not, of course, an assessment which was shared by the other prominent BBC victim of the Hutton report, Andrew Gilligan.

But if Dyke's show of support had given Ken a boost, then that day's *Evening Standard* brought him back down to earth, carrying as it did the headline 'Boris storms ahead in poll'. The YouGov survey, which – unlike the previous day's poll – specifically asked London voters to choose between the mayoral candidates, put Boris on 49 per cent, Ken on 37 per cent and Brian Paddick struggling on 12 per cent. It certainly indicated that the Lee Jasper affair had had a negative impact on Ken's campaign, and that Ken's attacks on Boris were failing to affect his ratings. The Boris campaign was as keen as ever to play down the idea that their man was so far ahead, welcoming the poll as 'encouraging', but pointing out that there were still forty-five days before polling day and that Ken would be 'tough to beat'. Ken's spokesman insisted: 'If the agenda of the election shifts to the key issues for London then Ken will win. There is still all to play for.' And, returning to their favourite theme of the previous ten days or so, he added: 'Boris Johnson was humiliated this week by independent experts confirming his transport policy is undercosted by £100 million a year.'

Undaunted, Boris got on with launching his housing manifesto at the Royal Institute of British Architects, expressing concern about the serious drop in the number of first-time buyers in London. He unveiled a scheme to be called FirstSteps Housing, through which 40,000 homes would be built and made available for 20 per cent less than similar properties to anyone paying income tax at the basic rate, with funding coming from the Regional Housing Pot. He also pledged to spend £60 million on renovating more than 80,000 empty properties in the private sector for people on housing waiting lists.

There were crime and environmental aspects too: more importance would be attached to 'designing out' crime, whilst Boris would use his powers to protect the Green Belt and historic views across the capital when considering planning applications. But he stuck by his early pledge to abolish the rigid target that 50 per cent of new homes should be 'affordable', instead insisting that he would work with the boroughs to ensure affordable homes were built. 'The out-of-date adversarial approach of Ken Livingstone has failed to deliver the housing that London needs,' he said. But Ken claimed in response that the policy would have 'devastating consequences' by 'pricing houses even more out of the hands of ordinary Londoners'.

Also that afternoon, it emerged that Ken was mounting a legal challenge against the closure of a large number of post offices in London. 'Communities in every part of London, especially the most vulnerable people, depend on their local post office,' he said. 'Post Office Ltd has not provided adequate time to consult on its proposals, leaving me with no alternative but to ask lawyers to seek leave to challenge their decision to close 171 post offices in London through a judicial review.' He didn't make much of this issue during the campaign – even though it would have been a popular and populist cause to champion – perhaps because he was completely at odds with the Government, which was pressing ahead with its programme of Post Office 'modernisation'.

Tuesday 18 March was the opening day of the formal campaign, and Ken hit the ground running by launching his re-election bid at the Royal Festival Hall, where he was flanked on stage by – among others – Doreen Lawrence, who had already spoken out against Boris. Ken gave a wide-ranging speech in which he talked about his own record on issues and contrasted it with Boris's inexperience. He also indicated that he was wary of fighting the campaign on the basis of personality but rather he wanted policies to be held up to scrutiny. 'This election is not *Celebrity Big Brother*,' he said. 'It is about the most serious issues and the future of our city. The stakes are very high.' Yet he attacked Boris on a range of fronts: he reminded his audience that Boris had condemned the Macpherson report; he claimed that Boris was 'the ideal person to lead us into the seventeenth century' on the basis of his support for nuclear power, and opposition to a smoking ban and the minimum wage; and he variously said that he posed the risk of 'wrecking' the city or 'bankrupting' City Hall if he made the wrong decisions on the big issues. 'There's a risk about everything with Boris. I'm not attacking his character, I'm attacking his judgement, which has been wrong on almost every issue,' was his damning verdict.

But, out on the campaign trail already himself, Boris responded to the attacks on his lack of experience. 'That's a bit rich coming from the man who presided over the collapse of Metronet and a bit rich coming from the man who presided over the loss of millions of pounds from the LDA and still cannot produce a full audit trail,' he said defiantly. As for the nature of Ken's campaign, he summed it up thus: 'He is basically rooted in a 1980s politics of division and playing one group off against one another.' Boris did, however, appear to come a cropper when he was interviewed by Andrew Neil on BBC Two's *The Daily Politics* that lunchtime, about his much-attacked bus policy. When Neil asked him the cost of it, he replied: 'Well, that depends on the development cost and various other factors that of course we will bear in mind.'

'So we don't know?' queried the presenter.

'We don't know the cost,' admitted Boris.

This prompted Ken to accuse Boris of 'incompetence' and called on him to withdraw his transport manifesto.

As Boris and Ken each painted the election as a battle with the other, Brian Paddick struggled to get a look in – as the opinion polls were demonstrating. He appeared to be clinging to the hope that people would ignore the two big personalities come election day. He supported this by falling back on the rather weak standby of local council by-election results, which showed that since he had been selected to stand for the Liberal Democrats in London, his party had in fact been beating both other parties. 'The only polls that matter are the ones on polling days and these show that the Liberal Democrats are winning across London,' he said, before making this incredible claim: 'The London election is a two-horse race – between me and Boris. The way the voting system works means I am the only candidate who can beat Ken Livingstone.' Observers concluded that this might have been an attempt by the Lib Dems to persuade Paddick himself that it was worth spending the next forty-four days criss-crossing the streets, halls and television studios of London – as no-one else was convinced by it.

Despite Lee Jasper's departure from City Hall, the effects of the police investigation into the LDA's funding of a number of groups connected to him continued to be felt. News came that a third friend of Jasper's had been arrested and questioned, this time Joel O'Loughlin, who ran the LDA-funded Diversity International. It was a sign that the affair was to continue to haunt Ken throughout the campaign.

The Green Party's candidate, Siân Berry, briefly stepped into the limelight the following day when she and Ken made a joint appearance at a nature reserve in Camden to pledge each other their second-preference votes. Whilst the second preferences of people voting for Ken with their first vote were going to be irrelevant, the redistribution of Berry's votes could prove vital to the race. The London Green Party had met two nights previously to officially agree the 'Siân 1, Ken 2' tactic, as an 'insurance policy' to prevent Boris from winning. The pair issued a joint statement in which they said that Boris's opposition to both the Kyoto treaty and the £25 congestion charge for the most polluting vehicles showed that he 'cannot be trusted with London's environment'. They also found common cause in supporting the retention of the existing congestion charge zone and the 50 per cent affordable housing target, and opposing all further airport expansion serving London.

But that day's *Evening Standard* was dominated by another Andrew Gilligan front-page exclusive, again related to leaked emails from City Hall. With Jasper out of the way, it was now Transport Commissioner Peter Hendy who was in the line of fire. Gilligan published emails written by Hendy which prompted accusations of him politically interfering in the mayoral election campaign, since a man in his position was barred from expressing political views. In one message, the Transport Commissioner wrote to Ken's chief of staff, Simon Fletcher: 'Is there mileage, now or later, in refuting Boris's two public transport ideas – artics [bendy buses] cause death by fire and crushing cyclists, and Routemasters are good?' In another he referred to fires on bendy buses as potentially being 'meat to BJ's campaign'. Among other allegations that Gilligan made was the claim that 'an informal discussion took place with TfL about setting up an "attack" unit within the organisation's press and public affairs departments to undermine Mr Johnson', although nothing ever came of it.

Boris was irate. 'This indicates that Transport for London is caught up in Ken's political machine, which is utterly inappropriate,' he said. 'This says more about the Mayor and the way he does business than anything else. Clearly they all think they are above the rules. It raises the question: can we trust what TfL says from now on?'

Hendy did not make a personal response of any kind, but a statement from TfL denied that there had been any breach of the rules on political neutrality. 'Misleading statements had been made about the safety of bendy buses. Peter Hendy is well known for his robust, factual defence of transport improvements in London,' it stated.

Ken's campaign, although on the back foot, tried again to pile the pressure onto Boris over his bus policy. 'The *Evening Standard* story today now places Johnson's unravelling transport policy centre stage,' said a spokesman for Ken, who accused Boris of trying 'to divert attention onto process to avoid the important story'.

That Wednesday night saw Paddick dart off to Daunt Books in Marylebone for the launch of his autobiography, *Line of Fire*. But why was he publishing it in the middle of the election campaign? He claimed that he would rather not have published it at that moment, telling the *Evening Standard*: 'I think, given the choice again, it could have been done differently, but I was bound by contract.' Observers of the contest couldn't decide whether his publisher was thinking that more copies would be sold because of his involvement in the election or that Paddick reckoned the book would help his electoral chances. Either way, it didn't seem to make any difference in the end.

On 20 March Gordon Brown publicly came out in support of Ken, despite a history of hostility between the pair. They went to Canary Wharf to meet community activists and East End residents with London Minister Tessa Jowell and the local MP, Jim Fitzpatrick. The Prime Minister heaped praise on Ken's record on transport, the environment, jobs and housing, describing him as 'an inspirational figure in London, a crusading Mayor, and one that has made a huge difference', which seemed almost to be overcompensating for his enmity towards him. Explaining why Brown had come out in support of him, Ken cited their agreement over the danger that David Cameron and the Conservatives posed. 'They're better looking than they were under Michael Howard, but beyond all the flim-flam, trivia and personality politics, on the serious issues that decide whether people will work or get a home, they haven't changed,' he said. Brown also put his name to an article in the *Standard* which again referred to Ken's record on getting the agreement on Crossrail, helping deliver the Olympics and tackling crime. 'The only choice for London must be Ken Livingstone,' he concluded.

Friday 21 March, Good Friday, marked the beginning of a few days in which the mayoral race fell out of the media spotlight over the long Easter weekend. Naturally, the leafleting, the canvassing, the campaign visits and the strategising all continued, but it wasn't until after the weekend that the campaigns hit the radar of the wider public again. Ken went straight back into the breach with a salvo on what appeared, by this stage, to be his favourite subject: the cost of Boris's bus policy. Now he was citing an independent transport consultancy, TAS, as having calculated that the cost of Boris's policy to introduce a new fleet of Routemasters was £114 million and not £8 million, and again called on Boris to withdraw what he described as 'a totally falsely costed transport manifesto'.

On Tuesday 25 March, Boris held a photocall outside Chelsea's football ground to highlight his 'Payback London' scheme, which had been launched in February. 'It's a good liberal principle of restorative justice and it will deliver benefits for people in London who are fed up with a minority of kids acting up on buses, causing fear and apprehension,' he said. 'I think it's absolutely vital we reconnect teenagers' rights to free travel with their responsibility to behave and not to cause a lot of aggro.'

There were also reports that Boris and his team were already in talks with individuals they were identifying as potential executives to run City Hall in the event of him winning the mayoralty. A few days later, the *Times* would report that Boris was chairing a 'transition team' to draw up a 'first 30 days' strategy. On the one hand it was essential that he did this so that he would be able achieve some quick wins if he did gain power on 1 May. However, any such talks would also open him up to accusations of being presumptuous about the result and really needed to be kept under wraps for the duration of the campaign.

On the back of gaining the second-preference endorsement from the Green Party the previous week, Ken sought to brandish his environmental credentials further with a separate environment manifesto. There was little new in the document, which he chose to launch in Richmond, where the Lib Dem-controlled council had introduced a ground-breaking policy of charging residents more to park the most polluting cars on the streets. He praised that move and urged Liberal Democrat supporters there to support him in the election, since it was a two-horse race between him and Boris, and his own environmental policies would chime with Lib Dems in a way that Boris's would not. Indeed, he branded Boris's environmental credentials as 'entirely fake', saying he was 'a throwback to another age'.

The next day, Boris went on the offensive again over the *Londoner*, during a visit to Valentines Park in Redbridge. He pledged that he would axe the publication and that the £1 million saved would instead be spent on planting 10,000 trees. More significantly, he gave an interview to *New Nation*, a black community newspaper, in which he promised that any administration he formed at City Hall would reflect London's 'wonderful diversity'. In remarks which had the potential to cause an internal Tory row over quotas or positive discrimination (but didn't), he said: 'I think if you've got equally qualified candidates [for a job], one black and one white, then for me I would want to appoint someone from a community that needs support and encouragement.' He also issued his most contrite apology yet for having used the terms 'piccaninnies' and 'watermelon smiles' in his journalism some years previously. 'It's taken me a while to realise that people were as upset as they were,' he admitted. 'Because I wrote those words in a way that was intended to be satirical, it's taken a mental journey to understand that actually there was offence given, and it does matter. But I do understand that now and I'm sorry.'

In advance of that evening's hustings at KPMG in Blackfriars, organised jointly by London First, CBI London and the London Chamber of Commerce and Industry, Ken laid into Boris over his plans to close the offices which the Greater London Authority runs overseas. 'Nothing therefore more clearly symbolises the difference between myself and Boris Johnson for London businesses, and the future of our city, than my opening offices to promote London in the US, China and India and Boris Johnson's pledge to close down all offices promoting London abroad,' he said. Boris replied to the attack by saying: 'For too long this Mayor has concentrated on his ego and foreign policy and less on the concerns of Londoners, and these offices are an example of this.' However, he then appeared to begin backtracking on his original pledge when he said that 'from day one I will review every office under a value-for-money programme', thereby leaving the option available of keeping them open after all.

The two principal rivals were joined by Brian Paddick and Siân Berry for the hustings, in front of an audience of about 400 members of the business community. None said anything especially spectacular or surprising, although there was one fiery moment when the issue of campaign donations caused a slanging match between Ken and Boris. Boris attacked Ken for failing to be transparent over the declaration of his donations, whilst Ken accused Boris of having accepted free office space for his campaign. Boris repeated 'wrong, wrong, wrong' as Ken made the claim and dismissed the allegation as '*Guardian* codswallop'. If Boris and Ken made the headlines, Team Paddick felt their man had clearly been the most impressive performer at this hustings, and were becoming increasingly frustrated at what they saw as the media's unwillingness to treat him equally with Ken and Boris.

Donations remained a live issue the following day – exactly five weeks before polling day – when the Electoral Commission announced its response to Greg Hands's complaint: there was no evidence that Ken had breached the law over the way donations to his campaign were being declared. He was ordered, however, to change the wording of the message on his website which was soliciting donations, to ensure that cheques were being written out to Labour rather than 'The Ken Livingstone Campaign'. Neither Boris nor Hands was happy with this outcome and Hands would raise the matter on the floor of the House of Commons before the end of the campaign.

That morning, two days after Ken had done so, Boris launched an environment manifesto, in which he contrasted the approaches that the pair of them took in finding solutions to the same issues. He said that his approach was about using carrots rather than sticks: encouraging people to do the right things for the environment instead of fining them for failing to do so. The centrepiece of his plans was to announce a scheme – similar to one called RecycleBank operating in the United States – through which households would be rewarded with vouchers in return for recycling waste, thereby reducing the amount sent to landfill. He reiterated his pledges on the Green Belt and tree-planting, promised to invest £6 million in making open spaces cleaner and said that he would work with the boroughs to encourage Londoners to install insulation in return for council tax rebates.

In the afternoon, Boris headed back to the Commons, where a debate was taking place on policing in London. It was at times ill tempered and Labour MPs goaded Boris, with Tony McNulty, the minister in charge of policing, dismissively referring to him as 'the honourable Gentleman representing somewhere in Oxfordshire'. Boris challenged McNulty to back his plans to use part of the Mayor's publicity budget on putting extra community support officers on buses, but the minister accused him of finding the money in 'some magical little pot' before letting rip. 'The slightest scrutiny would show that his [Boris's] overall spending plans are neither sustainable nor justified,' McNulty continued. 'He is as cavalier with the facts in that regard as he is in so many other aspects of his political life … Far too often, in all that he does in his attempt to be Mayor, he treats Londoners like idiots.' It was another sign that the Boris campaign was seriously rattling his opponents.

A report in the *Times* that day had not helped matters for Ken. According to close allies of the Prime Minister, it reported, 'Gordon Brown has all but written off Ken Livingstone's chances of winning the London mayoral election'. The piece went on to say that in Brown's circle it was felt that there was some consolation in that a Boris victory would be 'a disaster' for David Cameron. Downing Street later described the story as 'utter garbage' and, unsurprisingly, a spokesman insisted that Brown was confident Ken would win.

Meanwhile Paddick came under attack from, of all sources, the Green Party. The party's Assembly members, Darren Johnson and Jenny Jones, turned up at Liberal Democrat HQ in Westminster to deliver a letter to the party leader, Nick Clegg, expressing concern that there was no Liberal Democrat candidate standing in the election. It wasn't that Paddick had kept a relatively low profile that week but that he was departing from previously stated Lib Dem concerns about the environment on various of his policy platforms. Scrapping the low emission zone and opposing the £25 congestion charge on 'gas guzzlers' were two of his positions the Greens highlighted, suggesting that Lib Dem voters would do better to support Siân Berry instead.

Friday 28 March saw the official close of nominations for the contest, with ten individuals accordingly being nominated to appear on the London mayoral ballot paper. As detailed earlier in the book, some putative candidates had failed to get the signatures together, whereas others had simply decided that it wasn't worth standing when a £10,000 deposit was at stake.

But it was crime that dominated the day on the campaign trail, with Ken launching his policing manifesto the day after two more teenagers had been murdered on the streets of the capital. Seventeen-year-old Devoe Roach had been stabbed in an attack in Stamford Hill, whilst Amro Elbadawi, 14, had his throat slashed in Queen's Park – deaths which brought the running total of teenage murder victims in London during 2008 to eleven. Ken pledged to deploy extra resources to target the murders of young people, also prioritising drug crime, rape, domestic violence and defending London against terrorist attacks. He also pledged to continue reducing crime by 6 per cent a year, claiming credit for reductions already achieved by increasing the number of police officers.

When asked whether he felt in any way responsible for the latest murders, he replied: 'I do not feel responsible,' pointing to a general reduction in crime, but admitting that 'the only area we have got a serious increase is the tragic youth murders'. Paddick felt Ken's response was insufficient, saying: 'Livingstone has said there is nothing he or any commissioner of the police can do about it. If that's the case it's time for Livingstone to make way for a man that can.'

Boris, meanwhile, was scathing about the way Ken had condemned the media's reporting of these and similar murders on television the previous evening. Ken had told BBC London: 'You have a base pattern on TV, radio and newspapers that "if it bleeds, it leads". Sometimes I switch on and watch your programme and it's crime, crime, crime. I never switch on and see a headline saying "murder rate cut 28 per cent, rape down 25 per cent, crime falling five years in a row". You don't report the good news.'

The pungent phrase 'if it bleeds, it leads' comes from America, where violent crime often dominates local television news bulletins, but Boris was quick to condemn Ken: 'It is shameful that the Mayor complains that the media focus too much on violent crime in the capital. I call upon him immediately to withdraw his new catchphrase "If it bleeds, it leads". When kids are dying on our streets, his attitude is both chilling and dismissive.'

In a typically robust response, Ken retorted: 'I will continue to use the phrase until I start seeing on TV and in the papers a celebration of whenever crime is coming down.'

The tactic of launching sets of policies targeted at particular interest groups or sections of society was generally one of Ken's favoured methods of electioneering. But at a lunchtime hustings hosted by Age Concern, Boris took the unusual step of launching a manifesto aimed at older Londoners, *Appreciating Our Seniors*. He repeated pledges to protect the Freedom Pass and declared his intention to make the city safe for older people and to stop post office and hospital closures, which disproportionately affected older people.

There was also a further accusation from the Tories about Ken's funding. Greg Hands now claimed that the train drivers' union, ASLEF, had given £20,000 to Ken's re-election campaign in 2004, but that the money had never been registered with the Electoral

Commission. Again, the Labour Party denied that it had ever breached any rules.

Paddick, meanwhile, announced another American recruit to his campaign team, despite the election being only a month away. Jerome Armstrong, known in the United States as 'the Blogfather', where he had been one of those responsible for breakthroughs in internet campaigning, took on the role of web strategist, with a remit of getting Paddick's message out via new media.

The candidates spent their weekend covering all four corners of the capital between them, with Ken variously attacking the record of the Tories on the London Assembly for failing to back his budgets to increase police numbers and Boris for – you've guessed it – his bus policy.

Boris and Paddick both found time to talk further about tackling youth violence when they attended an event at the Damilola Taylor Centre in Peckham. Boris also dropped in on a Hindu temple in Neasden and later celebrated Newroz, the traditional Iranic new year holiday. He further underlined his commitment to the many communities in the capital when he repeated the promise he had made to *New Nation* about the need for a diverse administration at City Hall in an interview on GMTV's *Sunday Programme*. He also gave an early hint of his intention to form an administration of all the talents, adding that he had been approached by people 'from across the political spectrum' offering to help. And he set out what his initial priorities in office would be: 'What I want to do in my first hundred days is put in place measures that will appreciably make a difference to the quality of our lives and particularly safety on the buses, safety on the streets, safety on the Tube, suburban railway stations, areas for which the Mayor has direct responsibility, where people don't feel safe enough and we could do a lot better,' he said. Boris also added that he would continue to speak his mind if elected to City Hall. 'The people in London want someone who's going to speak his mind and speak up for them with passion about the things that matter to them, and that's what I want to do. I can't auto-lobotomise myself and turn myself into some other product, some pasteurised, homogenised, emulsified politician. I've got to keep telling it as I see it.'

The final day of March saw Boris – fresh from *GQ* magazine's assessment that he was the fourteenth worst-dressed man in Britain (a verdict surely reached before he was kitted out for the race) – officially launch his mayoral campaign. The location, a community hall in Edmonton, was significant, since three teenagers had been the victims of murders nearby in recent weeks. He was joined on the podium by Ray Lewis, his new friend from the Eastside Young Leaders Academy, and David Cameron, who acted as warm-up man for his old friend. Heaping praise on Boris, he described him as 'twice as charismatic' and 'twice as energetic' as Ken. 'I don't always agree with him but I respect the fact that he's absolutely his own man. He's a proper Conservative – practical, open minded and keen to get things done. And he's someone who has a properly thought-through plan to make London better,' said Cameron.

Boris painted a dismal picture of what he called 'the greatest city on earth' after eight years under Ken, setting out the clear choice as he saw it between another term ruled by a 'superannuated Marxist cabal' or the 'fresh approach' which he offered. He repeated his pledge to chair the Metropolitan Police Authority, promising to give a lead on tackling crime, and stated that his mayoralty would have two 'big and symmetrical' objectives: to advocate, promote and encourage the work of the voluntary sector and to persuade London's wealth creators to contribute more to the city's communities.

Ken was in Tower Hamlets to launch his housing manifesto, where he again emphasised his pledge that Boris was actively opposing – that 50 per cent of all new housing should be affordable.

'Unlike Boris Johnson's hotch-potch of gimmicks and impractical proposals, which would reduce pressure for new cheaper homes to rent and buy, my manifesto is a comprehensive plan for meeting the housing needs and preferences of all Londoners as effectively as possible,' he asserted.

Paddick, who was not scoring many hits in the traditional press, had clearly got his new web strategist to work straightaway. He announced that he would be the first-ever British politician to conduct an interview over Twitter – a text message-based social networking and blogging service.

The *Evening Standard* brought news of its latest YouGov poll, which gave Boris a 10-point lead over Ken. Boris was on 47 per cent, Ken on 37 per cent and Paddick was trailing on 10 per cent. In the run-off between the two main rivals, this would deliver Boris the mayoralty by 56 per cent to Ken's 44 per cent. Not for the last time, Ken's campaign issued a lengthy rebuttal of YouGov's methodology, describing it as 'fundamentally statistically flawed'. But Peter Kellner, president of YouGov, resolutely stood by his polls' findings, citing that in 2004 its final poll of the mayoral campaign had been less than one percentage point away from getting the result spot on.

The candidates were able to digest the latest poll on their way to that evening's debate, hosted by the *Standard*. It was a good, robust encounter but Ken made the news. First, in answering a point about the congestion charge, he confirmed that he would not raise the £8 basic rate. Secondly, he announced that if re-elected he would adopt Boris's 'Payback London' policy. When Boris protested at this theft Ken asked simply: 'What sort of idiot, when they hear a good idea, wouldn't take it on board?' He even proffered his own policies to Boris and asked cheekily: 'Would you like to meet President Chávez?' Ken's most passionate comments were reserved for the BNP. Keeping the BNP off the London Assembly, which he said would provide 'a platform in City Hall for their venom and their hatred and their intolerance', would matter more to him than whether he won or lost.

The three candidates clashed over policing. Ken argued that getting police back on the streets had been a deliberate, politically driven decision; it hadn't happened by accident, he said. He also claimed credit for the extra police, funded by council tax increases. They disagreed, though, over whether London was safer, Boris complaining that the Home Secretary had feared going out for a kebab in Peckham. 'That's because she doesn't know what's in it,' replied Ken. 'I want a London where the most dangerous thing in Peckham is the kebab,' Boris shot back.

1–13 April: A month to go

April began with Labour's deputy leader, Harriet Harman, pictured wearing a police stabproof vest to go out in her constituency in broad daylight. The picture caused a storm, both because it followed remarks from the Home Secretary, Jacqui Smith, in January that she would not feel safe walking around London alone at night, and because it undercut Labour claims that crime was falling. Harman was not alone in her embarrassment, though: a video of Ken Livingstone making what seemed to be some very unguarded remarks about his party turned up on the web. In what appeared to be a leaked out-take from a campaign video Ken was asked what his proudest political achievement had been; he responded cheerfully: 'Oh, it's taking on and smashing the New Labour machine in 2000, when Tony Blair wouldn't let me run for Mayor, and just grinding them into the dust … but you won't be able to use that one.' Two 'sad indictments' on the same day, according to the opposition, who each used the phrase to generate political capital from these slips.

The next day the embarrassment was Boris Johnson's, as he received a backhanded endorsement from the far-right British National Party. In a statement posted on its website, the BNP declared: 'In this race, the Tory clown Johnson is a lesser evil than the Marxist crank Livingstone, so replacing the latter with the former would, on balance, be an improvement for the majority of

Londoners.' Boris's opponents were gleeful, believing that it damaged his hopes of moving beyond the earlier controversies about his journalism. But the endorsement was anything other than enthusiastic and showed the BNP had a shrewd understanding of how to make proper use of the electoral system in London. It also had the effect of drawing the media spotlight to the party in a week when Nick Eriksen, its number two candidate on the Assembly list, had to stand aside after writing on his blog that 'women enjoy sex, so rape cannot be such a terrible physical ordeal'. Boris, anyway, immediately rejected the endorsement: 'I utterly and unreservedly condemn the BNP and have no desire whatsoever to receive a single second-preference vote from a BNP supporter.' He found himself in hot water, too, over old and apparently racist articles published in the *Spectator* when he had been editor, which had been unearthed by the black newspaper *New Nation*. They had been written by the *Spectator* columnist Taki and Boris could only apologise (again), 'I am sorry for what was previously written as it does not reflect what is in my heart', and attack Ken (again), claiming that he was resorting to negative personal attacks because he had nothing positive to say.

That evening's *Time Out* hustings provided the occasion for a minor row about who was hiding from whom. Ken's camp accused Boris of pulling out and suggested that he was ducking debates (he insisted he had never agreed to go). Boris responded by issuing a list of hustings he had attended, along with ten pages of campaign visits and events he had undertaken since October, and attacked Ken for pulling out of a couple of hustings himself. The event itself suffered from Boris's absence. It was rather a muted affair, with the only news being Brian Paddick's announcement that he would offer free travel for all full-time students in London.

The following day, 3 April, was probably the most extraordinary of the entire campaign. It had some normal moments, Boris making an announcement about his proposed alcohol ban on the Tube and bus network, and a new campaign poll by ICM putting Boris 2 points ahead in the run-off and 8 points ahead in the first round, 48 per cent to 40 per cent, with Paddick trailing on 10 per cent. There were normal moments in the papers' coverage, too, with a very critical Andrew Gilligan opinion piece in the *Evening Standard* headlined 'Now we're all counting the real cost of Ken'. Gilligan had become a major figure in the campaign, and just a few days later was to be rewarded with the prestigious Journalist of the Year gong at the British Press Awards. The judges praised 'relentless investigative journalism at its best from a man who has put himself back in the headlines for all the right reasons'. The award, though, was for his reporting and some of his peers questioned the wisdom of these heavily anti-Ken opinion pieces.

For all the normality, two bombshells dropped on the main candidates' private lives. The first concerned Ken. BBC London revealed that he has five children, by three women, rather than the two with his current partner who were publicly known about. He was described as an 'involved father' with his other children. 'I don't think anybody in this city is shocked about what consenting adults do,' he said. 'As long as you don't involve children, animals or vegetables, they leave people to get on and live their own life in their own way … There is a difference between private and secret. There is nothing in my private life that is not known to my partner, family or my close friends.' There were suspicions that he had leaked the news to the BBC because a forthcoming biography, written by a BBC reporter, Andrew Hosken, and due to be serialised in the *Daily Mail*, would have revealed it. The second admission came from Boris, who admitted to having smoked marijuana and taken cocaine. Interviewing him for the women's magazine *Marie Claire*, Janet Street-Porter suggested: 'You smoked dope before you went to university,' and Boris replied: 'That's true, but the stuff you and I may have smoked is not the same as what the kids are having now. I think skunk and this stuff is very, very dangerous.' He did say that he thoroughly disagreed with drugs but she pressed on, asking him about cocaine use. He replied: 'Well, that was when I was nineteen. It all goes to show that, sometimes, it's better not to say anything.' He had previously made jokey references to cocaine use, saying on *Have I Got News for You* in 2005: 'I think I was once given cocaine but I sneezed and so it did not go up my nose. In fact, I may have been doing icing sugar.'

Her Majesty's fourth estate in full cry is an extraordinary sight and the press leaped gleefully on both admissions, providing extra juicy titbits and endless reams of commentary. Of these, Amanda Platell's piece in the *Daily Mail* that weekend particulary riled Ken. She argued: 'The voting public surely has a right to ask the man who's seeking a third term as the Father of the City what kind of a father he has been to his own offspring … it's simply not credible to claim that these issues don't matter to voters.' Meanwhile Boris didn't help his cause by denying what he had just appeared to acknowledge, explaining: 'I was once at university offered a white substance, none of which went up my nose and I have no idea whether it was cocaine or not.'

After a tumultuous week on the campaign trail and with a month to go until polling day, that weekend's papers carried a lot of commentary, too. Most interesting was Iain Martin's piece in the *Sunday Telegraph*, because it reported dramatically raised expectations in Conservative HQ about the result. 'It would be hard to overstate the importance the Conservative high command places on victory in the London race,' he wrote, arguing that 'close will not be good enough'. That paper also carried an interview with Boris – one of few during the campaign, as many journalists reported difficulty in getting to sit down with him for any length of time. In the interview, Boris expressed his pent-up fury at some of the tactics used against him.

'I think he [Ken] will fight dirty,' he said. 'They are already doing blatant misrepresentations of our positions, just absolutely ruthless, going around lying about what we are offering. We are offering free travel for the elderly. They are literally going round houses, knocking on the door and lying.'

Whether or not they were lying, 'they' were certainly keen to damage him, and Tessa Jowell did her bit over the weekend, banning Labour ministers from referring to Boris by his first name only. From now on it would be either 'Boris Johnson' or 'the Conservative candidate'. 'What we have to avoid is a situation where people think this election is a joke and that the future of London is not serious ... our argument, made publicly at every possible turn, is that Boris Johnson's policies for London are not serious,' she said. Bearing in mind that most of the nation already referred to him simply as 'Boris' it did seem a case of closing the stable door after the horse had bolted.

Monday 7 April was a big day for the Liberal Democrats as Brian Paddick launched his manifesto, the party's 'Contract for London'. The main plank dealt with crime, Paddick promising not to stand for re-election if crime didn't fall by 5 per cent a year on his watch. And he received the endorsement of Duwayne Brooks, the friend of Stephen Lawrence who was with him on the night he was murdered. Paddick also promised to publish a comprehensive transport plan within three months, including his cross-river tram project and free travel for students; to convert London's 83,580 empty properties into sustainable homes at affordable rents; to turn London into the greenest capital in Europe; and to hold regular public meetings. He would be, he promised, the 'listening Mayor of London'. More immediately, though, he had to listen to a plea from the Labour think tank the Fabian Society for Lib Dem voters to give their second preferences to Ken. In an open letter to Nick Clegg posted on the *Guardian* website, the society's general secretary, Sunder Katwala, said Lib Dems should endorse Ken because he had a 'creditable record on several key Liberal Democrat concerns', unlike Boris. The plea was not warmly received. Meanwhile Ken himself was setting out plans for a major extension of the 20mph speed limit, into every residential street in London. Speaking to the road safety charity Roadpeace, he said he would work with the boroughs to introduce the new limits everywhere and then exempt some roads.

Boris had his own launch – of a document detailing Ken's broken promises on everything from preventing a rise in domestic violence to introducing a culture card. 'This just goes to show Ken Livingstone cannot be trusted to deliver on his promises,' Boris said as the campaign to neutralise Ken's perceived advantage on the experience front continued. Equally welcome for the Boris campaign was an intervention from David Cameron to sanction policy departures from the national line. 'It's very important that it's his manifesto, his proposals and his mayoralty,' he said. It was a significant moment, allowing Boris to go toe to toe with Ken as an independent thinker, operating above party politics. If it gave him a boost, the latest polling suggested he hardly needed it, though. YouGov now put him 13 points ahead – on 49 per cent to Ken's 36 per cent and with Paddick yet again a distant third on 10 per cent.

The next day had lots of launches, too: Operation Black Vote's anti-BNP campaign, the first party election broadcasts (PEBs), Brian Paddick's new website and a Boris pledge card. The Operation Black Vote event was an opportunity for Boris to repeat his anti-racist credentials and to repeat his charge that Ken was dividing people whilst he would unite them: 'The current Labour Mayor has run out of ideas and has concentrated on the politics of division rather than uniting people.' The Boris pledge card mimicked one of New Labour's most effective campaigning tools, distilling the candidate's message into a clear set of commitments: more police, tackling violent crime, safer transport, more recycling and cutting money spent on bureaucracy. The PEBs were very different from one another but very much reflected their campaign strategies: Ken focused on the big picture, a thriving London, Boris on the need for change, for 'fresh thinking and creativity and energy', and Paddick on crime. His was the hardest-hitting, with lots of black and white pictures and moody music to make the point that violent crime is a serious problem, and only he had the experience to tackle it. As well as the PEB, Paddick now launched his new campaign website, developed by his American web consultant, Jerome Armstrong, and his team. He said the team had 'injected a new momentum to our web campaigning, building on the huge support I've already been getting from Londoners on the web'. The website made use of some cutting-edge technology, and whilst it didn't mark much of a turning point for his campaign, it may have marked an important moment in British political campaigning on the web.

During the day, Ken faced a brickbat as he was accused of 'suppressing' the true cost of the Olympics. A former senior official of the Olympic Delivery Authority (ODA), Jack Lemley, claimed that the Games could cost more than £20 billion and that Ken had kept quiet about the soaring budget. The ODA, though, said that no-one else working on the project shared his view. Early that evening four of the candidates went to the No2ID hustings in Euston. Ken was absent, reflecting his support for ID cards. Boris took the opportunity to tie him, again, to an unpopular national Government: 'He is clearly embarrassed that he has toed his party's line and shown full support for ID cards from the start.' Boris's charge that Ken was hiding was rather less sustainable, as the three main candidates came together later that night for a debate on the BBC's *Newsnight*, hosted by Jeremy Paxman. It was an entertaining encounter, with both Ken and Boris on good pugilistic form, and it shed interesting light on some key areas of the candidates' policies. For Boris this meant the first proper examination of his Routemaster policy, and he didn't do well. Paxman began by asking about the reported estimate of £8 million for reintroducing Routemasters, and Boris claimed never to have uttered that figure. That, he said, was the estimated cost of putting conductors on the fleet of bendy buses. 'If you want conductors for the new generation of Routemaster buses, which I do and I think would be essential for London and would be much valued by Londoners, then you'd need to spend about twenty-five million quid,' he said. And what about the cost of the actual buses? 'They would cost no more and no less than the Mayor's own manifesto commitment to buy another 500 hybrid buses which are going to ply the streets of London, which will be bought, as the Mayor well knows, not by Transport for London but by the bus companies.' Still no figure, and as Boris ploughed on their host began the famous Paxman hassle: 'Give us a figure, come on.' 'What is the figure?' 'How much do you intend to spend on this new fleet of Routemaster buses? A figure! A figure! I despair.'

Eventually a response: 'I invite the Mayor now to tell us how much he is proposing to spend on the new 500 hybrid buses.' Boris clearly didn't know, and in rather an endearing act of desperation appealed to the man he was hoping to unseat for the answer. As Paxman moved on to talk to Paddick about his proposal for trams, Boris had one final bash at the buses. Paxman, rapier sharp, shot back: 'You've told us quite enough without a figure.' Within Boris's team, this encounter was considered the low point of his campaign.

Boris was not the only one to see his transport policies come under close scrutiny. Ken had the most public record, and his opponents raised both the danger of bendy buses and the western extension of the congestion charge. He, though, had a contentious answer ready on each of them. On deaths caused by bendy buses in particular he gave no quarter: 'Where they've killed someone it's not been because they were long. It's because someone stepped under them or there's been an accident ... We have about twenty-four people a year killed by buses in London, and if you're on a bendy bus you're half as likely to have that accident than if you're on a Routemaster.' Paddick asked about one particular accident and Ken was in no mood to stop now: 'I'll give you the answer. The answer is that the person who fell under the bus was several times over the legal limit for alcohol and he fell under the front of the bus and it would have happened to any bus, and his friend, who was also several times over the legal limit for alcohol, was so unaware of this that he walked away ... I'm afraid that the blood tests showed this person was completely, massively over the limit. He fell under the bus.' Blaming accident victims for their own deaths – whatever the truth of the matter – is not usually regarded as the best way to win friends and influence people, particularly during an election campaign, but Ken was clearly in no mood to alter the sometimes awkward and grating persona which had served him for the best part of forty years in London politics. It was the same on the western extension of the congestion charge. 'You can't run London on the basis that this bit opts out,' he said. 'I went into the [2004] election saying I would extend the zone.' But he did have words of consolation for those who feared he would raise the basic £8 congestion charge: 'If I break my word and increase the congestion charge for cars below the pollution level, I will resign.' Calling it 'environmentally trivial', Boris repeated his promise to ditch the £25 charge, backing Paddick, who had also called for its repeal.

The two main candidates may have taken the brunt of what Paxman had to unload, but Paddick did not escape. Paxman asked who they would vote for with their second-preference vote. Boris would say nothing; Ken said he'd already done a deal with the Greens but of the two there that night, 'without a moment's hesitation, Brian

Paddick'. Paddick was more qualified: 'I think Londoners are between a rock and a hard place, looking at these two candidates to my left.' Ken leaned across and asked gently: 'You've got a second preference, Brian, what's it going to be?' Paxman probed further.

'I haven't made my mind up,' replied Paddick.

'You can't choose between these two?'

'No, I can't.'

'You can't be serious. You think they're, what, equally bad or equally attractive?'

'I think they are bad in different ways.'

It was an awkward moment, because Paddick knew that as soon as he answered he effectively removed himself from any kind of serious consideration, but not answering also made him look foolish. It would not be the last time he was asked.

The candidates rowed, too, about Boris's experience of management in the private sector. Paddick interrupted to ask how many people he managed at the *Spectator* – twenty? At least fifty, replied Boris, pointing out that the 'Liberal candidate scorns organisations with fewer than fifty people'. He kept calling Paddick the 'Liberal candidate' and would refer to Ken only as the 'Labour Mayor', except on the one occasion when he slipped and asked: 'If I may just finish this point, Ken, or Kenneth, as I suppose I should call you.'

'You can call me Ken after all this time,' replied the Labour Mayor.

They also discussed the London Development Agency funding scandal, Ken claiming it was already being investigated before the *Evening Standard* began its investigations, and were asked by Paxman about the Mayor's salary.* Was it too high, too low, or about right? Boris thought it about right, Paddick a bit high; Ken thought it was

* £137,579 in the 2008/09 financial year.

about right, too, although he couldn't resist adding: 'It was only £80,000 when I first stood.'

'Well done,' replied Paxman sarcastically.

Aside from the questions each candidate had a chance to set out the main points of his pitch to voters. For Ken this was a chance to defend his record: 'I don't mind people saying "you can do better", but don't rubbish what has been a very good eight years.' As the debate came to an end Boris felt he had more still to contribute. 'Can I just say—' he asked.

'No you can't,' replied Paxman.

'Why not?'

'Because we're out of time, even for the three of you.'

The pair of them sounded like a bright but mischievous school-boy and the teacher he had pushed just a little too far and who was delighted to slap him down. This spirit of gentle childhood anarchy lived on in the best YouTube experience of the campaign: someone dubbed the voices from the *Newsnight* debate over archive video footage of the children's TV series *Rainbow*, with Ken as Zippy, Boris as the pink hippo George and Paddick as the uptight bear Bungle.

The *Newsnight* debate also touched on campaign funding, and it would not be long before Ken's answers came back to bite him. Ken, saying he would struggle to compete with Boris's massive war chest, again refused to divulge who donated to his campaign, telling Paxman that the donations went via the Labour Party and he didn't want to know personally. The next day the *Evening Standard* reported that during the 2004 campaign Ken had accepted a secret £30,000 donation from a property tycoon who wanted to build a theme park. It was another story from Atma Singh, by now well known to the *Standard*'s readers as the Mayor's former adviser on Asian affairs, and it appeared to undermine yet another part of Ken's carefully con-structed persona, that of a politician above being influenced by wealthy interests. Ken attacked both the story and the source (his campaign said Singh had been let go by the GLA for a 'failure to discharge his duties'). In the meantime both his opponents pounced, Paddick saying: 'I have always thought it improbable that the Mayor could remain in the dark over the identity of his funders and this appears to confirm my suspicions.'

If that day's papers brought bad news for Ken from the *Standard*, they brought better news in the form of an Ipsos MORI poll carried out for the Unison trade union, which put him on 41 per cent, Boris on 40 per cent, Paddick on 14 per cent and Siân Berry on just 4 per cent. After recent polls giving Boris a lead of up to 13 points it was welcome news for Ken, who said the election would be 'neck and neck', even if the poll had been conducted for a strongly pro-Labour group. Ken also announced plans for a new fleet of forty-four high-capacity trains on London Overground. It was a reminder of what he had been doing as Mayor: taking over the old and decrepit North London line and spending money to upgrade the trains and stations.

Strangely, for all this activity and with Ken and Boris both finding their campaigning stride, one journalist and ex-politician chose this moment to urge people not to vote. Writing in the *Times* that morning, the former Conservative MP George Walden told its readers that 'your duty is to stay at home. A mass abstention would show that Londoners have pride enough to want a different calibre of politico in charge. When democracy reaches the end of the line, the most democratic thing the public can do is to show they know.'

The next event, that evening, was the singular event of the campaign, and generated headlines and trouble for the candidates before it even began (trouble, at least, for Ken, who found himself the object of an attempted citizen's arrest by Brian Haw and other Parliament Square peace protesters, who accused him of trampling

their democratic rights). The event was the London Citizens'
Convention, held in Methodist Central Hall on 9 April. Neither
public meeting nor hustings, the convention was a fascinating mix
of churches, schools, trade unions and other voluntary and community groups. Rather than give the candidates the chance to speak at
length and respond in vague terms to questions from the floor, it put
very specific proposals, painstakingly worked up over several
months, to the four leading candidates and invited them to agree.
The proposal which had generated the headlines was turning
'Strangers into Citizens' by supporting an earned amnesty for illegal
immigrants. They had all agreed – less of a problem for Paddick,
whose national party was already committed to the policy, or Berry,
whose Greens adopted a laissez-faire attitude to these matters, or
even Ken, who had bucked the Government line so regularly and so
vociferously that they surely couldn't take offence at this latest mis-
demeanour. By putting Boris, though, in direct conflict with his
party – which explicitly rejected such a policy – it showed that he
was willing to take advantage of David Cameron's decision to sanction such departures. In the question-and-answer session Boris even
rubbed it in: to a chorus of heckles and boos from the trade unionists
and assorted left-wing activists in the hall, he was in full swaggering,
arm-waving form. Describing himself (incorrectly) as the grandson
of a Muslim immigrant from Turkey, he backed the proposal vigor-
ously, saying he believed his grandfather would be 'proud' of him for
standing on such a platform. It was a good example of what specific
questions to the candidates in such a personality-based contest could
elicit, what Boris's campaign would sign up for if necessary, and how
far the mayoralty (which has absolutely no powers over immigration
at all) had been transformed by eight years of Ken into a base for
campaigning on issues outside the Mayor's formal remit. If there had
been any doubts about that, they were swiftly assuaged when Boris

unblinkingly agreed to fund a unit to promote a 'living wage' around the rest of the country.*

Despite his joining the others in making these promises, the evening didn't appear to offer much for Boris. The presence of vocal whistle-wielding union activists and liberal churchmen hardly provided a welcoming environment, and sure enough, he did often find himself speaking against a chorus of boos. But each time that happened a request for calm came from the stage, reminding the convention that candidates should be heard politely and given the chance to speak freely. Boris was – and the audience were rewarded with more and more wordy, witty but nevertheless clear agreements to act. Among these was the extraordinary vision of a Conservative Party candidate for high office, a former member of Oxford's elitist Bullingdon Club, declaiming loudly that a central plank of his platform and one of which he was most proud was to be 'transferring money from the wealth-creating sector to transform the lives of these kids across London' – his proposal for a Mayor's Fund. In reality, the demands from the convention – particularly on crime, where the focus was very much on self-help and community involvement – were probably closer to Boris's vision for London than they were to Ken's. And the event was a marvellous one – getting away from interest-group politics and stage-managed party affairs, this was London's voluntary sector engaging with the candidates in a meaningful way. Andrew Gilligan, writing in the *Evening Standard*, noted later that 'these are the people the LDA should be working with'.

So by the time he came to speak on crime, after an extremely moving, impassioned and eloquent plea for action from a young girl whose brother had been stabbed to death just five months previously,

* The estimated wage necessary to allow someone to live decently in London. At the time of writing (May 2008) it was £7.25 an hour.

Boris had at least given the audience pause for thought. He didn't agree to every one of the convention's demands (his commitment to abolish the Mayor's free paper the *Londoner* was always going to make it hard for him to use it as an outlet for positive stories about immigrants, and no Conservative could realistically promise an end to dawn raids for illegal immigrants), but for all the unions' bluster and booing Boris performed strongly and received a warm ovation for his efforts.

Ken didn't come out of the event badly, either. As the only candidate who had been to the same event in 2004, he was able to receive the acclaim for meeting almost every one of the last convention's demands. Where he hadn't – on community land trusts – he had an answer that demonstrated a feeling for complexities and nuances, which presented a sharp contrast with the kneejerk tendency to agree from Paddick and Berry. Their experiences were also much as they had been throughout the campaign. Berry struck a sympathetic figure on the otherwise male-dominated stage and joked and pandered to the audience effectively. Paddick filled the role he had all the way through the campaign. He was like a school prefect, absolutely everything you could ask for: he said 'yes' more times and more enthusiastically than either Ken or Boris; he spoke passionately on crime and on social mobility; and he demonstrated enough understanding of the issues to impress anyone who was ticking boxes. But again, somehow, he failed to connect and he received the least warm applause of any candidate.

An explanation of sorts was on offer in the next day's *Evening Standard* and the following day's *Time Out*. Paddick was quoted in the *Standard* saying 'the more people know about me, the more they love me', but it was very different in *Time Out*. He gave an interview during which he ended up getting into a row with the reporter, Rebecca Taylor. He accused her of 'trotting out distortions and lies

which Ken Livingstone pushes out' and being 'totally unreasonable';
on his way out his press officer apologised and, noted the magazine,
so did he (eventually). In his autobiography Paddick talks about his
discomfort as a child in being an outsider, his difficulty in making
friends, and whilst he claimed in that book to have overcome those
early troubles and become a much happier person, anyone watching
his performances on stage could be forgiven for thinking otherwise.
This was curious since he could also be charming and witty, and he
was certainly interesting, thoughtful and prepared to buck his party
line when thinking about London's problems. He was still in the race,
but, as Jeremy Paxman had made plain during the *Newsnight* debate,
his most significant contribution now would be as a delivery mechanism for votes to either Ken or Boris.

The hustings season was now in full swing, and on 10 April the
candidates trooped to LBC's studios in west London for their first
radio hustings. It was to be hosted by Nick Ferrari, the former tabloid
journalist and longtime LBC presenter and one of the personalities
who had considered standing for the Conservative nomination. If his
sympathies were clear – he would later state in a newspaper that he
backed Boris – he was determined not to join the talk show host
James Whale and incur Ofcom's displeasure, and this encounter was
so impartially moderated that they picked Monopoly cards to deter-
mine who went first.* The winner was Boris, who by selecting The
Angel, Islington was closest to City Hall (3.3 miles). Ken chose
Oxford Street (4.7 miles) and Brian Paddick Leicester Square (3.6
miles). The candidates would face a Routemaster bell if they didn't
answer the question and a 'Mind the Gap' announcement if they
really stepped over the line.

---

* Whale was sacked by TalkSport on 6 May for expressing on air his support for
Boris, contravening Ofcom rules about impartiality.

Neither prevented a fiery encounter, with Ken digging up an article Boris had written in the *Spectator* the week after the 7/7 attacks and denouncing him for having 'smeared an entire faith'. Boris had written that 'the problem is Islam. Islam is the problem. To any non-Muslim reader of the Koran, Islamophobia – fear of Islam – seems a natural reaction, and, indeed, exactly what that text is intended to provoke.' But Boris was furious with Ken's attack, telling him that such comments 'demean this race and demean your office'. Ken in turn had to defend himself for having embraced Yusuf al-Qaradawi, who has endorsed suicide bombings against Israel, calling him 'a bitter opponent of al-Qaeda, and we need to talk to those Muslims who are opposed to al-Qaeda'. Ken also found himself on the defensive when it came to the revelations about his private life, which he refused to answer. 'I have a very good, happy extended family. We're all happy with the arrangement and I take the view that my kids have a right not to be in the public domain,' he told Ferrari. He criticised the columnist Amanda Platell, who had argued that knowing more would help them understand how he would run London. 'If you're unhappy with things I've been doing over the last eight years it's not going to be changed by the nature of the relationship with my family,' he said.

A number of other subjects stirred disagreement, too. Crime was the most contentious, Boris attacking Ken's claim that it had fallen by 6 per cent a year. (The next day he issued an even stronger, point-by-point rebuttal of the claim. Using statistics from City Hall press releases, he said people were now twice as likely to be mugged in London as in New York, with almost ten gun crimes reported every day in London and a 23 per cent rise in muggings of children under ten in 2006. He accused Ken of misleading Londoners.) Paddick also complained that the police's recorded crime figures give a misleading picture, which landed him in a spot of bother when Ken pointed out an apparent inconsistency: 'I'm sorry, Brian, but when you tell me about your great success of bringing down crime in Lambeth – and I agree – you used the same figures.' Paddick was also questioned about his working relationship with the Metropolitan Police Commissioner, Sir Ian Blair. He claimed that the de Menezes shooting was 'the only thing we fell out over … We have met since then and we actually got on very well. In fact for the last five minutes of the half-hour meeting he actually dismissed his notetaker. That's how much we trust each other. We both want to make London safer and we are going to work together to do that.'

Boris was on combative form, too, when the debate moved on to Ken's tearful apology for slavery, and on questions about his experience. He questioned the rationale behind Ken's contrition: 'I think there's a risk in having an unlimited cult of apology.' He wanted a culture which reconciles people rather than one which 'entrenches and feeds grievances', he said. He dismissed Paddick's argument that he lacked the experience necessary to be a successful political leader: Margaret Thatcher 'hadn't run a whelk stall before she became Prime Minister', he said. Ferrari's question about Andrew Gilligan provoked another angry exchange between Ken and Boris, Ken attacking the journalist for his role in the death of the Government scientist Dr David Kelly and Boris outraged by the attack. It was left to Paddick to provide the only moment of enlightenment: 'I was interviewed for an hour and a half by Andrew Gilligan and at the end of it he said he was a personal friend of Boris Johnson,' he revealed.

They did find some things on which to agree. After the previous weekend's fiasco when the Olympic torch came to London and demonstrators were repeatedly pushed to the ground by both the police and the accompanying Chinese security detail, they all thought it was a mistake to have the Chinese guards on London's streets, and they would all go to the Beijing Olympics. Would they have run with the torch, asked Ferrari. Yes, said Boris. 'There's an election on, I'd have run the whole way if they'd given me the choice,' replied Ken. The Mayor also provided an interesting insight into how he conducted his policy of engagement. Every time the Chinese asked for his advice on how to handle the Games, he said, he told them to 'do a deal with the Dalai Lama – that's your weakest point'.

Still, if the debate was fiery, it was not without its tender moments. At the start of the encounter, when Boris realised that there was a camera in the studio, he swiftly borrowed a hairbrush to smarten up his mop and Ken – in a picture which was widely reprinted – straightened his tie for him.

Later that day Boris was joined on the campaign trail by David Cameron. They went to Richmond, where Boris managed to totally overshadow his party leader – Cameron was gracious enough to acknowledge as much – and almost kicked him in the head whilst Cameron was in the middle of a television interview and Boris was scrambling onto a wall to address the throng. The following day it was up to Harrow, where Boris campaigned to keep Tube ticket offices open. TfL had plans to close as many as forty offices, largely because the introduction of Oyster cards had reduced demand for paper tickets, but Boris argued that there were good reasons to keep them open. Calling transport 'needlessly scary', he said: 'It's good to at least have a human being there to give a sense of security.' The clear if unstated message in both Richmond and Harrow was 'Ken doesn't care about people who live outside central London, but I do'. Paddick, meanwhile, was also out and about, arguing that many ethnic-minority voters felt let down by Ken and that he was very far from having their votes 'sewn up'. He got pretty short shrift from Ken's campaigners, who said the Mayor 'is not going to take any lessons from a person like Brian Paddick with virtually no record of taking a stand when the chips are down for ethnic minorities'.

As the Boris campaign gathered momentum he began to pick up support from the media, and not just the *Evening Standard*. Unsurprising were warm reports and interviews in the *Telegraph*, his alma mater. Its columnist Celia Walden dined with his father, Stanley, whilst Alice Thomson and Rachel Sylvester sat down with the candidate himself. 'I'm not some lobotomised hologram,' he told them; 'there isn't an old Boris and a new Boris, they're two sides of the same person. The serious Boris has always been there.' More gratifying for the Conservatives was an apparent warming from the *Sun*, which now began reporting regularly and enthusiastically on Boris's activities.

Elsewhere the smaller campaigns continued at a rather less elevated level, and on 11 April the Greens launched their manifesto and, a couple of days later, their election broadcast. The smaller parties were only entitled to one election broadcast whilst the three main parties had two, so they mattered. The Greens certainly had the most creative, all graphics and bright colours, whilst some of the really small parties with their even smaller budgets had to make do with rather more straightforward efforts. The Green manifesto focused on their core policies, promising free insulation for every London home and cheaper public transport, although there were also commitments on the living wage and more office space for small businesses.

Ken was out highlighting another of his transport commitments: this time buying the Croydon Tramlink from its operators for £100 million. This, he said, would save TfL £4 million a year and allow for better maintenance of trams and stations. Meanwhile the *Standard* carried yet another claim from Atma Singh about Ken. This time it was his admission that, whilst working for the Mayor and in what was supposed to have been office time, he had been working to get him readmitted to the Labour Party, drafting letters to Tony Blair, then Prime Minister, on behalf of potential Ken supporters. 'It didn't occur to me at the time that it was improper,' he told the *Standard*,

'but I now realise it was not something we should have been doing.'
By this stage another new claim was hardly going to cause a sensation,
but the cumulative, drip-drip effect of the revelations was surely
having an impact. Over at Boris HQ they had their own newspaper
scoop to deal with. This one was rather less damaging: the *Financial
Times* revealed that one of the Reuben brothers, who had publicly
clashed with Ken over the £4 billion Stratford City development
(Ken said the Indian-born Iraqi-Jewish brothers should 'go back to
Iran and try their luck with the ayatollahs'), had made a donation
worth £4,000 to Boris's campaign.

On 13 April, a national opinion poll reported in the *Sunday Times*
saw the Conservatives stretching their national lead over Labour to
16 percentage points, but the picture in London was nothing like as
clearcut. An Ipsos MORI poll in the *Observer* put Boris just 2 points
ahead of Ken on the day when thousands took to the streets of the
capital for the London Marathon – including a certain Brian
Paddick, who recorded a time of 4 hours 52 minutes. He was dis-
heartened by the response, confiding to his diary that he felt 'no
feeling of jubilation, just an overwhelming desire to lie down. Wait
for media interviews that never come. Do raise £2,000 for charity.'

14–20 April: Almost there

On 14 April, a YouGov poll for the *Evening Standard* showed Ken Livingstone making up ground on Boris Johnson. Although this poll, in contrast with Ipsos MORI's the previous day, showed the Conservative candidate with a lead of 6 points, this was a reduction by half over the previous week, with Boris now the first preference of 45 per cent of those asked (down from 49 per cent), but Ken now on 39 per cent (up from 36 per cent). Brian Paddick's rating increased by 2 points to 12 per cent, but with his second-preference votes now looking like dividing equally between his opponents, the poll still showed Boris beating Ken by 54 per cent to 46 per cent in the final run-off.

Despite the poll being published against a backdrop of a seem-ingly worsening 'credit crunch', which was causing increasingly painful headaches for the Government, Ken found himself joined again by Gordon Brown on the campaign trail that day. They visited a Sikh temple in Ilford, but whereas the sight of a mainstream Labour figure backing the maverick Ken might once have been reassuring, there were now surely question marks over whether Brown could be deemed to be helping or hindering his man's cause.

Boris meanwhile proceeded to launch his business and skills manifesto, highlighting his claim that crime costs businesses in the capital £1.4 billion per year. But the Ken camp seized on Boris's

pledge to 'fully endorse the representation of London overseas'. This, they said, was a U-turn on a previous pledge to close London's offices – the so-called 'Kenbassies' – in various key cities around the world.

Ken came under fire from the Conservatives, however, for choosing to 'focus on people who make the gossip pages and not the news pages' after issuing a list of twenty celebrities said to be giving the incumbent Mayor their support. The full list ran as follows: Damon Albarn, Bill Bailey, Banksy, Billy Bragg, Jo Brand, Tim Campbell, Antony Gormley, Phill Jupitus, Peter Kennard, Alistair McGowan, Jonathon Porritt, Vince Power, Tony Robinson, Prunella Scales, Arthur Smith, Ralph Steadman, Emma Thompson, Vivienne Westwood, Richard Wilson and Robert Wyatt. However, the veracity of the list was called into question after several of the names, including Campbell, Jupitus and Porritt, all denied their support for Ken.

Tuesday 15 April saw the three main contenders over in Canary Wharf for a hustings organised by Reuters. Boris was already coming under pressure to name some of those whom he would appoint to the big jobs in the capital, if elected. At the Reuters event, he said that he didn't want to prejudice the election's outcome and the positions of putative advisers or staff by naming them in advance. Some existing appointees may be retained, he indicated, although he conceded that a return to City Hall for Lee Jasper was unlikely. However, he did reveal the identity of one key adviser who would be helping to set up his 'Mayor's Fund for London' – American-born Bob Diamond, the president of Barclays plc. This prompted Ken's camp to hit the phones to the press and accuse him of being non-domiciled for tax purposes – a claim which was later unequivocally refuted.

At the hustings, Ken acknowledged the nature of his audience by speaking in pretty pro-business terms, as indeed he had throughout eight years as Mayor. Most of the rest of his remarks and responses to questions were pretty predictable: his line about Boris's hardest business

decision having been which restaurant to pick for lunch with *Spectator* colleagues was given an airing, to which Boris interjected – to a warm response from the audience – 'It wasn't easy, but I showed leadership!'

Ken did, however, manage to make one offhand remark which wouldn't have endeared him to the people of Belgium. Having talked about millions of Chinese people being able to afford to visit London in the future, Ken somehow ended up revealing that Belgian visitors to the capital spend the least of any nationality, prompting him to say: 'We could do with less Belgian tourists and more Chinese.' Boris – with his record of having offended towns and cities, rather than entire countries – interjected in mock outrage: 'Send him to Belgium to apologise!' The Conservative candidate also used most of his usual lines: reminding his audience that he agreed with Ken's once-held view that two terms was enough for any Mayor and stating that the only benefit to London of giving money to the European Space Agency would be if the current incumbent were to be propelled into orbit.

Crime again dominated the Paddick prospectus, but the Liberal Democrat was especially vicious towards his opponents. He accused Ken of doing his personal best to support *Time Out* magazine's 24-hour drinking campaign, but then, having condemned Boris Johnson as 'a joke' and 'a comedian', he mocked him for inconsistency over what he has said about his experiences of drugs, saying: 'In, out, in, out; it gives a whole new meaning to the hokey-cokey.'

After the hustings, Boris went to talk crime in Croydon and then in Queen's Park, at an event attended by the parents of Amro Elbadawi, a fourteen-year-old murdered there in March.

The power of modern technology in 21st-century political campaigns was brought to the fore when video footage came to light – recorded on a mobile phone by a Labour supporter – of Boris apparently admitting that replacing bendy buses with new-style

Routemasters with conductors would indeed cost £100 million. This was radically different to the £8 million figure he had previously given. Yet when questioned about it for a BBC debate hosted by Andrew Neil (Boris's ex-boss as publisher of the *Spectator* – and never thought to be his greatest fan), he stuck resolutely to the £8 million figure. He was later forced to issue a statement insisting that his proposals would nonetheless be cheaper than the £143 million that Ken's planned 500 hybrid buses would cost.

Later in the evening there was a hustings organised by the black community in Kilburn, conveniently enough on the day that Ken had chosen to launch a race relations manifesto, in which he promised to do more to have the staff of the Greater London Authority and its associated agencies better reflecting the ethnic composition of London.

The British National Party's Assembly candidates also had their lives subjected to close scrutiny by Andrew Gilligan in the *Evening Standard*, who found plenty to share with his readers. Apart from the party's mayoral candidate, Richard Barnbrook, who was reported to have once directed 'a gay porn film' (Barnbrook said it was 'a film dealing with sexuality; it was not porn'), there was Chris Forster, a full-time psychic who specialises in the use of the crystal ball. In what would seem to be inconsistent with the party's line on immigration, he was said to be married to a Chinese woman, whilst another of their candidates, Lawrence Rustem, was revealed to be half-Turkish.

Ken's association with the controversial Muslim cleric Yusuf al-Qaradawi had already attracted regular criticism from his rivals, and any further references to him were never going to be helpful to the Labour campaign. But the Ken camp had to endure another day of it when the preacher's face appeared on the front page of all editions of the *Standard* on 16 April alongside one Azzam Tamimi, under the headline 'Suicide bomb backer runs Ken campaign'. The paper

alleged that a group called Muslims4Ken was being run by, among others, the Palestinian-born and Hamas-supporting Tamimi, who had 'praised suicide bombers' and 'said he would volunteer for a suicide mission in Palestine'. Also in that day's *Standard* was an interview with Paddick in which he called Ken a 'nasty little man' and Sir Ian Blair a 'Stalinist'. The only person he had warm words for, in fact, was Boris, whom he called 'somewhat eccentric but otherwise really harmless as an individual'.

Boris, meanwhile, was the only one of the three main candidates to turn up to a hustings organised by the Centre for Social Justice, the think tank founded by ex-Conservative leader Iain Duncan Smith. Ken was accused of snubbing London's voluntary sector, whilst Paddick did not escape criticism, having apparently only decided against attending at the last minute. During an online chat for the *Sun*, there was a rare glimpse of 'the old Boris' – who had a view about everything and was not afraid to share it. Boris managed to get himself embroiled in the issue of the smoking ban, something which is not under the jurisdiction of the Mayor in any case. Responding to a reader who was angry about the ban, he said: 'If I had my way, we would have an online referendum in London about whether to give boroughs back the power to give discretion over smoking to pubs and clubs.'

A new set of crime figures allowed the leading contenders to battle it out as to who could talk tougher. Boris emphasised his plans to put an extra 1,500 police on the streets and ban the consumption of alcohol on the Tube, whilst Ken – visiting Peckham – called for tougher sentencing and bail conditions for anyone caught carrying weapons.

That evening, Ken went about courting the gay and lesbian vote at Heaven, the nightclub near Charing Cross, and a series of bars and pubs in Soho. With a fortnight of campaigning remaining, Paddick

opted to entertain journalists at a trendy art gallery, imploring them to give him a chance and asking them to consider that his two opponents were 'high-risk candidates'. 'I don't trust one because of what he's done and I don't trust the other because of what he's not done ... Don't write me off,' he pleaded.

The big story of the day two weeks before polling day was that the Metropolitan Police Authority was apparently suppressing publication of a report into the handling of the shooting of Jean Charles de Menezes at Stockwell station until after the mayoral election. The delay was due to the possibility of 'people making political capital out of it', an MPA spokesman was quoted in the *Standard* as saying, although the MPA later absolutely insisted that there had been no suppression; the report could not yet be published as it had not yet been completed. Still, it was an open goal for Ken's challengers. 'The only reason to delay this report would be if it were critical of the Commissioner and by association the Mayor, bearing in mind Ken Livingstone's unswerving support for Sir Ian Blair,' concluded former policeman Paddick, who branded the delay a 'disgrace'.

Yet it was trivialities which again dominated the day as the trio of candidates were back in a studio together for a live on-air hustings organised by BBC Asian Network. The event began with only Boris and Paddick in attendance as Ken was said to have been delayed on the Tube. His story changed, however, when he finally arrived half an hour late. 'I'm very sorry, but my kids haven't seen me any evening this week, and they didn't see me at the weekend, and they just wanted a little bit of time this morning. Sorry about that,' he told the presenter, Nihal Arthanayake. 'I left the house late – the kids don't understand why Daddy spends more time with Boris than with them,' he added. The difficult question of race then provided one of the more memorable quotes of the campaign, from Boris. He courted controversy by replying to the question 'Are you down with

the ethnics?' with the answer: 'I'm down with the ethnics, you can't out-ethnic me, Nihal.' Having already discussed his Turkish heritage, he added: 'My children are a quarter Indian, so put that in your pipe and smoke it.' It was another typical moment of candour from Boris, the like of which his campaign team were constantly hoping he would avoid. Paddick did not see the funny side, and reacted sharply: 'Sitting next to an Asian presenter and saying he can "out-ethnic" anyone just shows how stupid an intelligent man can be.'

As if that hadn't caused enough panic for those hoping to contain Boris's gaffes, the comments he had made the previous day about smoking required a clarification and then proceeded to provoke claim and counter-claim from his opponents. Boris issued a statement in which he said:

> Personally I do not like smoking and believe that pubs and clubs are better places since the ban came in. My point was that I believe laws like the smoking ban should have been decided at a local level rather than a national level. This is entirely consistent with my previous stance on the subject. It is not within the power of the Mayor to have a referendum, nor will I be lobbying for the power to grant one.

All very well, but he also had to confirm that he had been paid to speak to the Association of Tobacco (incorrectly referred to by him as the Tobacco Association) in June 2007, which resulted in a chorus of abuse from his opponents. 'London wants a Mayor who understands the importance of the ban on smoking in public places and supports it, not one who in reality opposes it and supports ways of getting round it,' said Ken, whilst Paddick asked: 'How can Londoners trust someone who has received money from the tobacco industry to be objective about the smoking ban?'

Ken, meanwhile, found the time to launch another specialist manifesto, this time for London's youth, in a further visit to Kilburn. His youth manifesto – or 'New Deal for Young People', as it was branded – was still being pushed the following day when he visited Camberwell with the Schools Secretary, Ed Balls. The Labour effort to support Ken really was pulling in the big guns now: apart from the Prime Minister's appearance at the beginning of the week, Foreign Secretary David Miliband had been out with him in Palmers Green a couple of days before as well. The incumbent Mayor was at pains to contrast his plans for centrally expanding facilities for young people with Boris Johnson's proposal of a 'Mayor's Fund for London', which would see business and the City being encouraged to donate into a fund to support community projects. 'Boris Johnson's plan that our young people should have to depend on charitable handouts from the City of London for the investment they need is a throwback to Charles Dickens's nineteenth-century world and would be doomed to fail and disappoint them and the local community organisations who need support,' claimed Ken. 'Once again he shows himself to be living in some past era and ignorant of how to plan and deliver proper services in a 21st-century city.'

But Boris retaliated himself, insisting that the money Ken had been talking about distributing was 'Government money that would be spent on London's young people, whoever is Mayor after 1 May. He is deliberately trying to mislead Londoners.' The Conservative candidate continued: 'On his watch millions of pounds earmarked for youth projects has gone missing or has been spent with nothing to show for it … Ken Livingstone's record is one of increased child poverty and more young people being the victims of crimes including muggings and murder.'

The gloves were well and truly off, and the Ken camp hit back at Boris again, unearthing some of his old newspaper columns which hinted that he favoured the dismantling of the welfare state and introducing charges for patients using the NHS.

The announcement later in the day that the RMT union was calling a Tube strike for forty-eight hours in the days running up to election day caused a further angry exchange between the two leading candidates. Boris called on money donated to Ken's campaign from three unions, the TSSA, the RMT and ASLEF, to be returned and highlighted the sixteen strikes which had taken place since Ken became Mayor. 'Ken Livingstone should put London ahead of his old-fashioned and outdated union paymasters,' he said. In return Ken claimed that the number of Tube strikes had reduced since he became Mayor and suggested his opponent was both 'ignorant' and 'incompetent' to talk about returning donations from the RMT since it ceased to be affiliated to the Labour Party 'years ago'. Either way, the threat of strike action was swiftly lifted and commuter chaos, which could have dominated the final days of the campaign, was averted.

Attitudes to homosexuality were in the spotlight on Saturday 19 April, when the three main candidates – along with Siân Berry of the Green Party and Lindsey German of the Left List – attended a hustings organised by Stonewall, the lesbian and gay rights organisation. Earlier in the campaign, Paddick had been the only candidate to attend the Stonewall annual dinner. When asked if he felt he 'had the gay vote sewn up' by a reporter at that event, his response was brusque: 'Why should I? The LGB community is a lot more sophisticated than to just vote for someone because they are gay.' Nonetheless, he started with a distinct advantage among a Stonewall audience.

Historically, Ken's credentials with the gay community were very strong, but he came under fire at this event for his links with Yusuf al-Qaradawi, who had previously called for gay people to be killed. Ken's simplistic response, that all major religions have problems with homosexuality, did not wash. Boris was attacked in turn for his stance on Section 28 and for having once equated civil partnerships to 'three men and a dog' getting married. But he did raise the spirits of the meeting when he announced that 'half' of his campaign team were gay. He won round even more doubters when Andrew Pierce of the *Daily Telegraph* pointed to his recent comments about 'out-ethnicking the ethnics' and asked him whether he could 'out-gay the gays and admit to a gay sexual experience'. 'The answer is ... [a long pause] not yet!'

Further evidence that the race was on a knife edge came in the following day's *Sunday Times*. A poll of 1,000 Londoners by Mruk Cello made it too close to call between Boris and Ken, with the former a single point ahead, leading by 45 per cent to 44 per cent. Paddick trailed on 9 per cent and the gap between the two frontrunners closed yet further after the distribution of second preferences. The candidates used the poll, and other stories in that Sunday's papers, to wind one another up as they prepared to face one another yet again, this time on BBC One's *Politics Show*. The exchange was a vigorous one, although the only really new story came when Paddick said he wouldn't be giving his second preference to either Ken or Boris – amazing since this was the only way his vote would influence the final result. At the end the presenter, Jon Sopel, asked them to describe each of the others in one word. 'Stale; got some interesting things to say about policing,' said Boris dismissively. 'Someone who's guaranteed that this has got the attention it deserves in an election; ... and Brian is someone I'd love to have working on my team if I'm re-elected,' said Ken, in rather more than two words. Paddick, as usual, kept to the rules and gave the wittiest and sharpest response: 'Tragedy; comedy,' he said. As they left the BBC all was clearly to play for as observers followed events in what would – on the wider political stage – be Gordon Brown's most uncomfortable week since taking office as Prime Minister (although there have been several more since).

21–30 April: The final countdown

The last full week of campaigning began with an air of mystery and anticipation. Boris Johnson's campaign team had organised a visit for their man to Manor Studio Ballet School in Clapham, where – in the words of their press release – he would be accompanied by 'a very special guest'. Rumours circulated as to who this might be, but then it emerged shortly before she was due to arrive that she was pulling out on account of feeling unwell. The 'she' in question was none other than Kate Hoey, the independent-minded Labour MP for Vauxhall, who most Tories think would sit far more happily in the Conservative Party because of her views on a whole range of issues. So the mere fact that she was due to have appeared on a campaign visit for Boris convinced many, on both sides of the political spectrum, that she was about to declare her support for him and defect to the Tories – or at the very least be thrown out of Labour.

But when contacted by the *Daily Telegraph*, Hoey vehemently denied any such suggestion with the following explanation: 'Boris told me last week he was visiting the ballet school – it's a great project so I said I would try to go along, like I would for any politician who wished to see a project in my constituency. It never occurred to me people would consider it an endorsement. It really pisses me off that I am being asked if I am staying on as a Labour MP – it's stupid, stupid, stupid.'

However, the Vauxhall MP pointedly refused to say whether she would be endorsing Ken Livingstone. 'I'm a Labour MP and I'm not endorsing anybody,' she said. Her reason for not attending the Boris event in the end was that she had 'a very bad chest', although that morning she did visit the Health Professions Council and by all accounts seemed to be in fine fettle. Boris, meanwhile, joined in the speculation about Hoey's personal views by saying: 'I think a lot of London Labour MPs are secretly hoping for a change of regime on 1 May.'

Ken's big set-piece event of the day was the launch of his arts and culture manifesto at the Institute of Contemporary Arts. Various celebrities from the world of showbusiness were engaged to back him, including the singer and activist Billy Bragg and the ex-*Coronation Street* star Shobna Gulati. Lots of worthy projects were included in his manifesto, such as a new open-air cinema by the Thames, support for a bid to host the 2014 Gay Games, an expansion of the existing programme of free festivals, and a promise to change planning rules to protect live music venues. Andy Burnham, the Secretary of State for Culture, was also on hand to lend his support – the fourth Cabinet minister in a week to do so.

But Ken was coming under fire again from his old foes at the *Evening Standard*. Andrew Gilligan's latest front-page story was headlined 'Ken's adviser is linked to terror group'. It claimed that until 2001, Dabinderjit Singh, a member of the board of Transport for London, had been a member of the International Sikh Youth Federation (ISYF), a group which was proscribed under British law. 'I was a sympathiser of the ISYF but the only time I came into the limelight with the ISYF was in 2000,' said Singh. 'The organisation was put up for proscription about two months later. When an organisation is proscribed, it's the organisation, not the individuals, that are banned.' It was another relatively tenuous link between Ken and a 'terror group', but the cumulative effect of such headlines on the campaign would be felt. In particular almost everybody who works in London, whether or not they read the paper, would have seen the negative headlines on *Standard* billboards across the city, and Joy Johnson on Ken's team certainly felt that this was the most damaging aspect of the paper's campaign.

Elsewhere in the paper, the latest YouGov poll had Boris leading Ken by 7 points: 44 per cent to 37 per cent on first preferences. Brian Paddick was trailing on 12 per cent, and Boris was predicted to lead by 6 points after redistribution of second-preference votes.

Meanwhile, Boris took the opportunity to name more of those whom he would appoint as advisers in the event of him winning the election to add to the sole name he had already announced, Bob Diamond. The advisory team who would oversee his fabled 'Mayor's Fund' – which would see donors funding a variety of voluntary-sector projects – would include Sir Trevor Chinn, Lord Marland (the treasurer of Boris's mayoral campaign), Richard Sharp, Wasfi Kani, Ray Lewis and Sir John Beckwith (uncle of it-girl Tamara). Many of those names would have meant little or nothing to the ordinary voter, but it was a sign that Boris was giving serious consideration to how he would implement his ideas if elected and that he was preparing for that eventuality.

That eventuality came a small step closer the following day when he received the endorsement that most politicians crave: a supportive editorial in the *Sun*. Britain's best-selling newspaper – which had famously done for Neil Kinnock in 1992 and then been the paper 'wot won it' for Blair in 1997 – was throwing its weight behind Boris. Attacking Ken for his desire 'to go on and on', reiterating the allegations of sleaze at City Hall and attacking some of his policies as 'pointless' and 'crackpot', the paper's readers were urged to back the man whom it believed to be 'smart and bursting with ideas'. Deriding Ken's campaign as 'stale and exhausted', the paper concluded: 'Boris Johnson has the energy and imagination to give this great city what it needs … A new and fresh Champion for London.' Such endorsements are generally as much a sign of what a paper thinks its readers are already thinking as they are an instruction to vote a certain way, but nonetheless, it was greeted with some excitement in the Boris camp and he was afforded a trip on the *Sun*'s open-top bus that day to boot.

He had also given an interview to the paper, published that morning, in which he highlighted his desire to seize money earned by drug dealers in the capital and use it to assist the police in the fight against crime. 'These crooks are making a fortune by peddling drugs, using the cash to buy luxury homes, flash cars, jewellery, plasma TVs and whatever else,' he said. 'London police should know that when they seize such assets they'll be allowed to use it to the benefit of Londoners.' The police were already getting a proportion of such money as a result of the 2002 Proceeds of Crime Act, but he complained that the Home Office was taking far too large a share.

This prompted Labour to issue one of its regular rebuttals aimed at Boris, accusing him of being soft on crime. On this occasion, the party claimed that he had specifically voted to water down the procedure for confiscating assets in a Commons division in July 2002 and pointed out a quotation from his book *Friends, Voters, Countrymen*, in which he justified his voting record on the Proceeds of Crime Bill by saying that the Tories had 'argued consistently for decency and humanity, while Labour accused us of being soft on criminals'. Tony McNulty, the Home Office minister responsible for the police, accused Boris of being 'out of touch and soft on crime. Even though people in London are concerned about gun crime, Boris Johnson voted against automatic five-year sentences for people carrying illegal guns,' he added. What he said may have been true, but Boris was the one making the running.

The latest allegation from Andrew Gilligan in the *Evening Standard* was again related to alleged links between Ken and a banned terrorist organisation. He had spoken the previous Saturday at a meeting in Harrow organised by the British Tamil Forum, said to be a front for the Tamil Tigers – the separatist Tamil group which is banned in Britain. The Sri Lankan High Commissioner in London, Kshenuka Senewiratne, had apparently written to Ken expressing concern at his intention to address the group, but had never received a reply, according to his spokesman.

Elsewhere in the paper was a further suggestion that the politics of race and ethnicity were causing clashes between the campaigns. The website of Muslims4Ken was reported to be using distorted quotations from Boris to minimise support for him among the Muslim community, by taking words out of context or even quoting articles which had appeared in the *Spectator* under his editorship but which had been written by others and bylined as such.

There was briefly speculation that Paddick was considering giving his second preference to Boris on the back of an article in the *Times* suggesting he would happily work for him, under the headline 'I could work with Boris but I couldn't trust Ken'. Paddick was quoted as saying: 'I just don't trust Ken Livingstone. The thought of having him as my boss sends shivers down my spine. I think Ken is getting very tired and is running out of ideas and as a consequence he is allowing his unelected team of advisers to dictate what happens in London. He is no longer engaging with the men and women in the street.' When asked if he would consider chairing the Metropolitan Police Authority if asked to do so by Boris, the Liberal Democrat candidate's reply – 'he hasn't put it to me' – led the paper to speculate that he would consider taking it. But Paddick swiftly moved to deny the story and put out a statement saying that his two rivals were 'as bad as each other and I would never serve in either of their administrations'.

The issue of the cost of the Olympics also came up again, as a result of a report by the House of Commons Public Accounts Committee which said the estimated cost of the Games had almost tripled since the bid was originally made. This gave Boris the chance to take another sideswipe at Ken, claiming that he had 'lost control of the budget for the 2012 Olympics'.

Yet Ken took the opportunity to go for Boris that night in a televised ITV London debate. It was arguably the rowdiest debate so far and Ken ridiculed Boris's plan to replace the bendy buses with a new generation of Routemasters. 'No-one will design one because people would be liable to be sued by the relatives of people who fell off the back and died,' he said. 'You used to have double figures every year for people falling off the buses.' Boris dismissed Ken's accusation, claiming that bendy buses were 'twice as dangerous as any other bus', although as with many of the debates between the three contenders, Ken's eight years in the job and mastery of the policy details enabled him to sound more authoritative than his rivals.

A minor diversion from the Boris-v-Ken battle came with the news that Respect MP George Galloway had been attacked with a rubber stress ball whilst out campaigning for his party's London Assembly candidates in an open-top bus in Holborn that afternoon. 'It hit George on the left side of his head, on the temple,' said an aide. 'He was momentarily dazed and because of the impact of the blow he lost his balance and hit the other side of his head on the side of the bus. There is a nasty bruise on the side of George's head, but he will continue campaigning.' The next day Galloway faced another assault, this time verbal: 'I salute your indefatigability… you w****r,' shouted a heckler from the street, mocking Galloway's infamous remarks to Saddam Hussein. This assault prompted, according to the *Sun*, a furious response from the Respect leader.

Wednesday 23 April – St George's Day – saw most watchers of

politics focusing on events in Parliament, since the Government was forced to make a humiliating announcement of compensation for those affected by the abolition of the 10p tax rate before Gordon Brown faced a fractious House of Commons at Prime Minister's Questions. But Boris was out on the campaign trail bright and early, celebrating the feast day of the patron saint of England with a trip to Smithfield Market for a traditional full English fry-up. He also gave an interview to the *Evening Standard* covering a number of different policy areas, but putting an emphasis on his desire to tackle social breakdown, particularly in the poorest parts of London. Having evidently familiarised himself with areas of the capital with which he was previously unacquainted, he said that he wanted to use the Mayor's powers 'to champion disadvantaged kids and give them opportunities, and to champion the voluntary sector working with them. I want to join up the two halves of London, to be a sort of human bridge between the great wealth-creating sector and the real anger, disaffection and disadvantage in the surrounding communities.' Helping the worst off was 'very much part of the attraction of the job', he added.

Boris really appeared to show a hunger for the role and acknowledged that he had to keep on the straight and narrow. 'This is by far the best thing I've ever tried to do,' he said. 'In so far as I have to be disciplined and committed and all the rest of it, I will do that. I know that I simply cannot afford to give the media any sign that I'm not taking it seriously.' However, there was in fact a brief suggestion of financial sleaze on Boris's part that very day, as Labour MP Karen Buck referred him to the Parliamentary Commissioner for Standards over his failure to declare the extent of his shareholding in a television production company, Finland Station. He owned one third of the company's shares, yet had not registered this fact in the Register of MPs' Interests – as he should have done, since he owned more than

15 per cent of the shares of a single company. Buck cried 'hypocrisy and incompetence', but Boris admitted responsibility for the 'oversight', he moved to correct the register and no-one thought any more of it.

However, on the subject of Boris's potential to cause problems for David Cameron and the Tories nationally, there was a fascinating contribution to the *Daily Telegraph*'s Three Line Whip blog later in the day from Iain Martin, the paper's head of comment. He reported that the Shadow Cabinet had spent 'a significant amount of time' at its meeting that week discussing what kind of relationship the Conservative leadership would have with Boris if he won. 'Apparently, it became clear in the course of the meeting that a top priority is to find ways of insulating Cameron's team from the fallout if Boris hits trouble of any sort once he is in office,' he wrote. 'A degree of distance will be required between the Westminster front bench and Boris, the Shadow Cabinet was told.'

Meanwhile, the *Financial Times* speculated about the position of Steve Norris in the event of a Boris victory. It suggested that he would be keen to run the London Development Agency, which Norris had described as 'the most dysfunctional body that most of us can think of'. The two-time former mayoral hopeful was also full of praise for the strategy being pursued by Boris's campaign. 'If you asked me what I'd do differently to 2004, this time around I'd go for the consolidation of outer London boroughs, where Tory support is strong,' he said. As for Boris's refusal to say who he would be appointing to various roles in the event of winning, Norris again commended the position he was taking. 'I think he's been well advised because he's not ended up with hostages to fortune … there's an adage that the only people who want detailed policy are the press and the opposition. Boris has observed that.'

Ken's big event of the day was the launch of his bus manifesto.

Aside from improving the reliability and cleanliness of the vehicles, he pledged to invest in hundreds of new more environmentally friendly hybrid buses and to double the number of bus stops with second-by-second information on expected arrival times. He also took another swipe at Boris's plans to get rid of the bendy buses and introduce a new fleet of Routemasters with conductors. 'This policy is an uncosted farce,' he declared. 'It is one of the most incompetent and fraudulent policies ever put forward by a candidate standing for public office in Britain – and is symbolic of the incompetence of the entire Boris Johnson campaign.'

At the launch, Ken made a clear attempt to distance himself from the Labour Party and the Government – on a day when they needed all the friends they could muster. Asked whether he felt his ability to win a third term was being hampered by a nationally unpopular Labour Government, he replied: 'It doesn't matter what party label I wear, I've always been an independent. When I came back into the Labour Party, the deal I did with Tony Blair was "you give me the money and I will spend it in a way that I think is right for London without the Government telling me how to do it".' In some ways, it was an extraordinary claim for a candidate to be making, but in reality, Ken was acknowledging what everyone else was thinking: that in the political environment in which he was seeking re-election, no-one selling themselves as the candidate favoured by the Labour Government would be onto a winner.

Making ambitious promises which you know you'll never have to keep is easy when you know you'll never have to implement them. That accusation could have been levelled at Brian Paddick by his opponents, had they been bothered to give his latest announcement the time of day (which they did not). The Liberal Democrat candidate cheerfully announced that he would turn London into 'the world's first wi-fi capital', with free wi-fi internet access to be provided 'in all public places in London'. The scheme, Paddick said, would be piloted in ten inner London boroughs before being rolled out across the whole of Greater London. He estimated the cost of the entire scheme would be between £36 million and £48 million, but that it would be cost neutral, since he would pay for it by abolishing the advertising and communications budgets of TfL.

The following day – a week before London's voters would go to the polls to deliver their verdict – saw Ken countenancing the possibility of defeat for the first time. It was the splash in the early edition of the *Evening Standard* and some saw it as a deliberate tactic: shoring up his core vote by showing his vulnerability and dangling the possibility of a Boris mayoralty before his voters' eyes. Speaking on the campaign trail in Lewisham, he revealed what he would do if he was defeated: 'If I don't win, come 6 May I will be taking the kids to school and starting a book on my last eight years as Mayor,' he said.

And that wasn't all. He went on to suggest how Boris should tackle the job if he was victorious. 'My advice would be: don't rush to make rapid change, try to take your time … and actually organise a more graduated transition.' Ken even joked that if he did lose, it would really only entail a job swap with Boris, since there would be a vacancy on the after-dinner speaking circuit.

But that wasn't the only report to emerge of candid remarks emanating from Ken's lips. He had also told a hustings organised by Christian groups at St Martin-in-the-Fields church that his support for the Olympics coming to London was nothing to do with the sporting competition, but because it had been a way to 'ensnare' the Government into funding developments in the city. 'I didn't bid for the Olympics because I wanted three weeks of sport,' he admitted. 'I bid for the Olympics because it's the only way to get the billions of pounds out of the Government to develop the East End, to clean the soil, put in the infrastructure and build the housing.' But he also seemed to admit, responding to suggestions from Paddick that they were mere 'guesswork', that the original costings published for hosting the 2012 Games had been deliberate underestimates. 'It wasn't a mistake, Brian. It was exactly how I plotted it to ensnare the Government to put money into an area it has neglected for thirty years. I am delighted that there will be billions of pounds from the Government. That was exactly the plan. It has gone absolutely perfectly.'

That morning had also seen a surprising piece of news in the *Guardian*: Ken's re-election campaign had been 'secretly' taking advice from his old foes Tony Blair, Alastair Campbell and the pollster Lord Gould. It reported that their advice had been sought by Tessa Jowell. Blair was said to have told her that the election was 'very winnable' although Ken would not be able to win solely on his record in office, but rather would have to 'align his experience with a vision of how he and Londoners will together continue to create the greatest city in the world' and be 'unambiguous that he will continue to attract private sector investment to the capital'.

During the day, the big campaign themes of transport and crime were the subjects of claim and counter-claim from the two main camps. Firstly, Andrew Gilligan at the *Evening Standard* had obtained leaked documents and emails which suggested that Ken had lied when promising to keep bus and Tube fare rises in line with inflation. A TfL plan which Ken had approved in the autumn of 2007 apparently proposed Tube and bus fare increases of 1 and 2 percentage points above inflation respectively in 2009 and 2010. However, Ken had told a press conference at the end of October that there would be 'no need' for above-inflation fare rises, a claim he repeated to the London Assembly a fortnight later and was still appearing to echo during the mayoral campaign itself when promising that 'fares will continue to be held down'.

Leaked emails from TfL's finance director, Steve Jones, and the

Transport Commissioner himself, Peter Hendy, added to Ken's difficulties. Jones had declared in an email to Hendy and others that he
was 'bemused' by Ken's statements, which were 'not compatible with
the assumptions we have made in our plans'. Hendy, meanwhile, had
written that Ken was 'adding stories' on fares. The Boris campaign
immediately fired off a press release accusing Ken of being 'arrogant
and out of touch', although Ken's spokesman insisted that the board
of TfL had adopted a business plan in January 2008 which took into
account his policy of not allowing fares to rise above inflation for the
following four years.

Secondly, on the subject of crime, Boris was joined by David
Cameron at Lambeth's Police Support HQ, where he accused Ken of
having 'lost control of crime'. He trumpeted his plans to introduce
New York-style crime-mapping, which he said was 'a proven tech-
nique for improving public safety'. But Boris's tough talking on
fighting crime was severely undermined when it emerged that
Richard Barnes – the Conservative group leader on the London
Assembly and a member of the Metropolitan Police Authority – had
made comments to the *Local Government Chronicle* which seemed to
suggest that safer areas would not get the same coverage of neighbourhood policing as they were currently enjoying. 'Some wards you
would term as "safe", yet they have full safer neighbourhoods teams
[SNTs] twiddling their thumbs,' he told the publication. 'Two miles
down the road, similar-sized teams are rushed off their feet ... At the
moment there is a commissioner and mayoral edict that SNTs
shouldn't be abstracted from their wards. There should be a core
number within each ward but they should be a borough resource.' He
had apparently claimed that this would form a 'major plank' of Boris's
community safety policy. The Home Secretary, Jacqui Smith, was
indignant. 'Boris Johnson can talk all he wants about tackling crime
with new websites but no words will compensate Londoners for the

loss of their police on their streets … he is a risk to our safety – a risk that Londoners can't afford to take.'

Boris was swift to issue a rebuttal. 'Richard Barnes's comments do not reflect my policy on policing whatsoever,' he insisted. 'I made it clear in my crime manifesto that I support safer neighbourhood teams, and I have absolutely no intention of changing how they operate.'

That evening, the three main rivals met for another television debate, this time on a special edition of the BBC's *Question Time*. It was a major occasion and all three candidates turned out with full retinues of supporters and hangers-on. They were treated to an entertaining evening. Ken was the most outspoken. David Dimbleby asked him about his recent comments on the Olympics: 'You make it sound like a con trick.' 'It was,' said Ken, who went on to repeat much of what he had already said about getting investment into east London. Brian Paddick did not perform strongly and, as Boris and Ken dominated affairs, his campaign team at one point grew so frustrated they stood up and waved at him to interrupt. When Paddick did interrupt Ken, complaining that 'this is a naked attempt for you to try and win second-preference votes from me', the Mayor simply shot back: 'Absolutely! Of course I want the support of Lib Dems.' For Boris the programme had its good and bad moments. He certainly managed to make his point about being independent: 'Any Mayor of London is going to have to bang the table with any Government,' he said. 'I would gladly embarrass any Government that is in power if it was in the interests of Londoners.' But in the short term it was he who would be embarrassed, by a question from the audience about morality. Dimbleby pressed him on his affair, and with his wife, Marina, and parents-in-law sitting in the audience, his response was awkward and embarrassed. When the end finally came he headed straight for Marina and after a few moments together he seemed to visibly lift.

The following day was less eventful, with the campaigns sticking to their predetermined plans of action. Ken and Siân Berry launched a joint attack on Boris's environmental policies. They stated their agreement on six key policy areas: support for the Kyoto treaty on climate change; backing the £25-a-day congestion charge for so-called gas-guzzling cars; commitment to the full roll-out of the low emission zone to cut pollution from lorries; opposition to airport expansion; support for 50 per cent of new homes being affordable; and maintaining the current congestion charge zone. By contrast, they claimed, Boris agreed with none of the proposals, whilst Paddick supported only two of them. Ken did not pull his punches in his personal attack on Boris. 'Boris Johnson is an environmental vandal, whose main contribution to environmental policy was as a cheerleader for George W. Bush's disastrous decision to oppose the Kyoto climate treaty,' he said. 'It didn't seem possible six weeks ago, but Boris Johnson's environmental policies have got even worse during the course of the campaign … last week he revealed that his "big idea" for London is to build a new airport in the Thames Gateway.' The pair reasserted their intention to give each other their second-preference votes – although it was universally acknowledged, of course, that the second preferences of Ken's supporters were never going to come into the equation when the votes were counted on election night. Indeed, Berry as good as admitted defeat in her assertion that 'to cast your second-round vote for a candidate who won't be in the second round is the same as not using it at all. Don't abstain in the second round – you have to choose between Livingstone and Johnson.'

Ken himself was the subject of a character assassination direct from Conservative HQ, with Chris Grayling, the attack dog of the Shadow Cabinet, joining Boris and some of the party's London MPs outside City Hall to publish an eighteen-page document, *The Case against Ken Livingstone*. It answered a series of claims made by Ken and his supporters about his record on crime, transport and offering value for money and – in Grayling's words – 'lays bare the scale of abuses that have taken place in City Hall over the past eight years'. He continued: 'Londoners are fed up with Ken Livingstone, who has become tired, stale and mired in maladministration ... he has spent vast amounts of money on building up a personal support structure for the Mayor which would do the dictator of a banana republic proud.'

That afternoon, Ken also came under fire during an adjournment debate in the House of Commons initiated by Greg Hands on the innocent-sounding subject of 'election candidates'. Hands used the debate to launch an attack on Ken, who was still refusing to declare the identity of any of the donors to his mayoral campaign. Ken had been cleared some weeks previously by the Electoral Commission of having breached any rules for channelling donations through the Labour Party. Hands argued: 'The Electoral Commission has farci-cally allowed a situation in which no Londoner can have any idea who is funding the campaign for the incumbent candidate for the position of London Mayor ... Five million electors deserve to know who is paying for all the glossy leaflets that come through their doors.' The topic was of particular relevance that day as it had emerged that trade unions with members working on the Tube had given in excess of £100,000 to Ken's re-election campaign.

The final weekend before polling day saw the two rivals executing different approaches to the campaign. Boris opted to tour the London boroughs, meeting voters on the ground. Starting at Billingsgate Market on the Saturday morning, he took in various high streets across the capital and had meetings with representatives of the Polish and Ghanaian communities, as well as finding time to visit an animal home in Kensal Green. Ken, on the other hand, appeared to take a rather grander approach to it all. He was joined on the campaign trail in Islington by Bertrand Delanoë, the recently re-elected socialist Mayor of Paris, and also released endorsements from Klaus Wowereit, the Mayor of Berlin, Gavin Newsom, the Mayor of San Francisco, and David Miller, the Mayor of Toronto. On the Sunday Ken appeared at an anti-war rally near Brick Lane, releasing the names of yet more celebrity backers from the peace movement, none of whom (apart from Dame Vivienne Westwood) were exactly household names. Was the support of Ed Simons of the Chemical Brothers, Chas Smash of Madness or Beardyman going to influence anyone's votes? It was only a few days before we'd find out.

The last three days of campaigning before voters went to the polls began with what, on the face of it, ought to have been good news for the Boris campaign: the penultimate YouGov poll for the *Evening Standard* put their man 11 points ahead of Ken on first preferences (46 per cent to 35 per cent) and had him retaining a lead of 10 points once second preferences were taken into account, suggesting he would win by a margin of 55 per cent to 45 per cent. Whilst the Livingstone camp branded the poll's findings 'farcical', the headline 'Boris surges ahead in poll' was not what the Tory strategists wanted to see either. Any indication that the mayoralty was in the bag would only serve to persuade wavering Boris supporters that their vote would not be vital after all. Arguably the most important figure for the campaigns to seize upon was that, when forced to choose between one of the two main candidates, 13 per cent of people remained undecided.

Ken's campaign was then accused of using 'dirty tricks' as part of a last-ditch effort to garner votes. Firstly, there was another attack on Boris's views on Islam, with the British Muslim Institute (BMI) issuing a Bengali-language leaflet which claimed that he hated Muslims. According to a translation reproduced in the *Standard*, the leaflet stated: 'Boris has expressed his hatred against Islam, the Koran and the Muslims … It is Muslims' moral duty to support Ken,' although the reverse side of the leaflet in English apparently did not include the same attack on Boris. The Conservative campaign released Bengali leaflets of their own to counter this. Secondly came the suggestion in some Labour campaign leaflets that the Freedom Pass – which offers free travel for the over-sixties – was 'under threat should a Tory or Lib Dem get into City Hall', a suggestion which the Conservatives claimed was also being spread by Ken's supporters when speaking to voters on the telephone.

Boris was incandescent. 'Dirty tricks like this play on the most vulnerable in our society and it is a disgrace that Ken's campaign will stoop so low,' he said. 'I support the London boroughs, who give free travel to the over-sixties, and I will work with them to extend it to operate twenty-four hours a day – a pledge the current Mayor has failed to deliver on.' As for the BMI leaflet, he described it as being 'more than sleazy. It is actually dangerous and is misleading people about something of sacred importance.'

The official Ken campaign stepped up its attack on Boris by unveiling a poster with the slogan 'Imagine Boris Johnson in charge of London's £39 billion transport budget. Suddenly he's not so funny'. However, Ken was still chirpily suggesting that he would offer his Tory rival a job in his administration if he won a third term, saying: 'I would genuinely want Boris to come in, take a job and get some experience.' Ken also unveiled the last of a series of mini-manifestos aimed at specific sections of the London electorate. At this eleventh hour, it was time for a manifesto for women. Whilst promising to make transport safer for women and to ensure that they got an equal share of the jobs which the Olympics would bring to London, he also called for tighter regulation of lap-dancing clubs and a crackdown on the trafficking of women into prostitution.

Boris secured an endorsement of his own that day from Brian

Cooke, the chairman of London TravelWatch, the official watchdog (funded by the London Assembly) which represents transport users in and around London. Cooke accused Ken of arrogance and having 'paid lip service to real consultation', concluding that after having met Boris, he thought he would make an 'ideal Mayor'. This intervention was not uncontroversial, however, with Ken's campaign saying that it was a clear breach of the rules about controversial political activity being undertaken by members of London TravelWatch.

Meanwhile, there was also something of a fiasco back at City Hall, which had to be evacuated due to flooding and a loss of power. A water main had burst in nearby Tooley Street, causing water to seep into the basement, where the building's café, media suite and a number of meeting rooms are located. The electricity to the building was switched off and there were fears – unfounded as it turned out – that the announcement of the election result on the Friday would have to be made elsewhere. Nonetheless, it prompted lots of jokes about leaks in the building and it being 'sink or swim' time for the candidates.

That evening, the three principal contenders took to the stage together for a final debate in front of the television cameras, aired live on Sky News and LBC radio, and hosted by Sky's indefatigable political editor, Adam Boulton. Challenged again about his position on the Freedom Pass, Boris had prepared a good line to make his case: 'We're all passionately in favour of the Freedom Pass, around the clock, on all modes of transport – not least because there's only one candidate eligible for the Freedom Pass before you tonight, ladies and gentlemen, and that's the distinguished gentleman on my right,' he said, referring to 62-year-old Ken. 'And I want him to be free to travel on the buses around the clock in perfect security and tranquillity from 2 May,' he added. Boris also taunted Ken with the words he had uttered in 1998 about how a Mayor should only serve two terms because 'that office inevitably became corrupt or corrupted' if an incumbent remained in office for longer. 'Ken, nothing you have said has persuaded me that you were inaccurate in your initial analysis,' said Boris. 'I think your office is tragically fulfilling your own prophecy.' But Ken hit back by saying that he decided to stand for a third term after seeing George W. Bush succeed Bill Clinton as American President, suggesting that the world would be 'a lot safer' if Clinton had been allowed to seek a third term.

The following day saw the return of Labour's Kate Hoey to the fore. After her no-show at a Boris campaign visit two weeks earlier, you might have thought that she would have kept out of the fray. But no, in a final campaign interview with Nick Ferrari on LBC, Boris revealed that the Vauxhall MP and former Sports Minister would be 'the first member' of his administration, serving as a non-executive director advising him on sport and the Olympics. 'If I am lucky enough to win she will be working on an agenda that includes protecting playing fields, boosting sports clubs and making sure that London's kids all benefit from the Olympics,' he said. 'Kate has a huge and well-known commitment to sport and to London, and I am determined to bring talent from across politics and the community to a new administration,' he added, in what was something of an echo of Gordon Brown's effort to create a so-called 'government of all the talents' the previous summer. Hoey, for her part, issued a statement that Boris was wrong to claim her as potentially the first member of his administration, but that she would serve him as a non-partisan adviser. 'This is not an endorsement of Boris Johnson for Mayor,' she continued. 'I will be voting for my party and Labour candidates on Thursday. I am a Labour MP and I am standing for Labour at the next election. I support the Labour Government, I have and shall continue actively to campaign for Labour in these elections.' Observers noted, however, that she had not explicitly stated an intention to give Ken her first-preference vote.

There was one further significant last-minute development to come out of Boris's interview with Ferrari. Throughout the campaign, Brian Paddick had been promising that, if elected, he wouldn't seek a second term in office if he failed to cut crime by 5 per cent each year during his first term. Ferrari managed to talk Boris into more than matching Paddick's pledge. The exchange went as follows:

> *Nick Ferrari*: If you don't cut crime by 20 per cent in four years, would you give me your promise that you wouldn't run again?
>
> *Boris Johnson*: I certainly won't run again if I haven't made a massive reduction in crime.
>
> *NF*: What's a massive reduction?
>
> *BJ*: I intend to exceed 20 per cent. There you go, Nick, will that do?

It was an unscripted, unplanned commitment, which Ferrari and others would look forward to holding him to in the event of him winning.

Those developments aside, there was little to report during the final forty-eight hours of campaigning, except that the candidates sought to shore up their support by reinforcing the messages they had been pushing for months on end. Ken was still on the offensive about Boris, distributing postcards with the message 'Don't vote for a joke – vote for London'. Deeming him 'unfit to do the job of Mayor of London', Ken listed 'a series of astonishing blunders' which Boris had made during the campaign and claimed that polling evidence showed him (Ken) to be the candidate who best understood the problems facing London. His campaign also published a highly tenuous and wordy complaint it was making to the Market Research Society about the methodology involved in the YouGov polls being used by the *Evening Standard*. It certainly had a last-throw-of-the-dice feel about it, as did the press release pumped out by the Ken campaign with more names of Z-list celebrities who were supporting him.

Boris's eve-of-poll messages encompassed a mixture of positive and negative campaigning. He emphasised his key policies of tackling gun and knife crime, boosting the police presence on the streets and putting more uniformed officers on Tubes and buses, and making spending at City Hall more transparent. But he too focused on his key opponent, claiming in viral emails that 'Gordon Brown and Ken Livingstone will think they can get away with anything and never be held to account' if Ken won his third term. His conclusion was: 'If Ken Livingstone wins on Thursday, it is another four long years of waste, deceit, scandal, cronyism, crime and congestion. He will revert to form, nothing will change and Livingstone and Labour will think they can continue to ignore Londoners' real concerns.'

Brian Paddick wrote a piece in the *Standard* in which he attacked both his opponents, Ken for having deceived voters and Boris for lacking experience. He urged people to use their first-preference vote for him but – with an air of resignation about his own inevitable defeat – advised them: 'With your second-preference vote you can vote tactically to make sure the wrong guy does not get his hands on City Hall.' As ever, he refused to say in whose box he was putting his second cross, although he would reveal after the event that it went to the far-left candidate Lindsey German, representing the Left List. When Ken found out, on election night, he told his opponent: 'You campaigned like a Tory and voted like a Trotskyist.'

The day before polling day, Boris came under attack in several newspapers. Unsurprisingly, the Labour-supporting *Daily Mirror* revealed under the headline 'Boris exposed' what it called 'the right-wing face behind the Joker Johnson façade', listing a series of reasons why people needed to vote for Ken in order to 'save London from Tory Boris Johnson'. The second salvo came from a more unlikely source: the *Daily Telegraph*, the paper for which Boris had been a star columnist until very recently. Whereas the paper had already given the Tory candidate its official endorsement in an editorial, Simon Heffer, its associate editor and another popular columnist, wrote a devastating attack on Boris, for whom he had worked at the *Spectator* and whom he had known for twenty years. Describing Boris as 'an act' rather than a politician, he wrote: 'The act is calculated and it has required serious application and timing of the sort of which only a clever man is capable. For some of us the joke has worn not thin, but out.' Heffer went on to condemn him for being 'pushy', 'thoughtless' and 'indiscreet about his private life' as well as having 'a blinding lack of attention to detail', adding that 'the guiding theme of his life is the charm of doing nothing properly'. Concluding that all three main candidates for Mayor were 'preposterous figures', he was only able to join George Walden in urging 'a massive abstention'.

Meanwhile, in a final campaign interview with the *Standard*, Ken was again seriously contemplating the idea of losing. 'If I lost, it would not be because we lost the argument,' he opined. 'It would in part be because the Tories would have run a superior campaign and in part because of differential turnout. Older voters who tend to vote Tory are three times more likely to vote than younger people, for example.' He did, however, seem to be clinging to the hope that the polls were overestimating Boris's support and that people would not bring themselves to vote for him once the stubby pencil was hovering over the ballot paper at the polling station, what some had dubbed 'hovering pencil syndrome'. 'I just think that although people may be toying with the idea of voting for Boris, when it comes to it they will find they just can't do it. This is too serious for that.'

But the paper printed a full-page editorial on page thirteen in which it declared that 'honesty and competence are the overriding issues' in the mayoral election. 'Democracy cannot properly function if our elected representatives have not proved themselves to be the guardians of integrity. Ken Livingstone has comprehensively failed that test. Londoners should vote for change and make Boris Johnson Mayor,' readers were urged. It was not long before they would begin giving their verdict.

Election!

When the candidates woke up on the morning of 1 May, they did so to an uncertain political future. Ken Livingstone and Boris Johnson both had an enormous amount riding on the outcome, but they were not the only ones. Their respective party leaders, Gordon Brown and David Cameron, also had huge stakes in the outcome. It would be the first time the leaders had faced each other in a significant test of public opinion since the Conservative leader (and his Shadow Chancellor, George Osborne) had bested Brown during the previous year's conference season – which had effectively served to stop Brown from calling a general election. But however unfamiliar it all was – all but one of the quartet were new to their role since 2004 – some things remained the same. The mayoral candidates pottered along to their local polling station bright and early, photographers in tow, to cast their ballots: Ken in Cricklewood and Boris, accompanied by his wife Marina, in Islington. Brian Paddick also rolled up at his local polling station in Vauxhall for the cameras, although he had actually already voted by post. The newspapers carried endorsements and commentary on how they thought their readers should vote. None of it was particularly surprising except for the *Guardian*, which, having criticised the *Evening Standard* for its bias, now carried the most extraordinary article in its G2 section. Headlined 'Be afraid. Be very afraid', it helped its readers to imagine 'what it would be like if this bigoted, lying, Old Etonian buffoon got his hands on our diverse and liberal capital'. Well, there would not be too long a wait to find out, but in the meantime the candidates and their supporters had another twelve hours or so for ritual 'get out the vote' efforts as they waited for the close of polls and then, more tantalisingly, for the counting to start on Friday morning.

That morning the *Standard*'s first edition reported: 'Boris ahead in polls, but it's so close.' A YouGov survey put him on 43 per cent of first-preference votes to Ken's 36 per cent, with Boris predicted to win in the run-off by 53 per cent to 47 per cent. All day the three major parties' headquarters were buzzing with news about turnout and likely results in the local elections across the country. The feedback to the HQs meant that at 10 p.m., when polls closed and taxis bearing members of the Cabinet and Shadow Cabinet began arriving at media outlets around London, many of them already had a pretty good idea of what the night would hold. Yet in truth no-one really predicted the extent of it: a woeful night for Labour, with the party slumping to its worst election result for forty years, and an extraordinary night for the Conservatives, gaining hundreds of councillors across the country. At 1.30 a.m., when the BBC broadcast its estimated share of the vote, the Conservatives were on 44 per cent, the Liberal Democrats on 25 per cent and Labour in third place on just 24 per cent.* As the same taxis which had ferried politicians into radio and TV studios took them home again after a long night of explaining away bad results and exulting in good ones, all eyes began to turn to London. And with results like this elsewhere in England and Wales, the possibility that Boris might have enough votes to win

---

* The BBC's predicted national share figure is a prediction of what the result would have been if the whole country had been voting in the local elections. It is based on a sample of about 900 representative 'key wards' from around the country.

began to dawn on Labour politicians who didn't appear to have considered it seriously before. They returned home with worried looks, in marked contrast to their opposite numbers in the Conservative Party: after long years of terrible results and false dawns on local election nights, finally they had real reason to smile – and hope.

The smiles were still there the next morning, fittingly enough the feast of St Boris (at least in the Bulgarian Orthodox Church). At 8.30 counting began at three centres – Alexandra Palace, ExCeL in Docklands and Olympia. It very quickly became clear that whilst Ken had done better than the Labour Party nationally, his performance was unlikely to be good enough to give him the third term he craved, since a record high turnout across London was being recorded – and, crucially, some of the highest figures were being recorded in the Tory-voting outer boroughs. In what looked like a repeat performance of the 2006 borough elections, the voters seemed to be turning out for the Conservatives again.

As the day progressed, initial returns prompted rumours that Boris might take more than 50 per cent of first-preference votes and win on the first ballot. Senior Conservatives were keen to downplay the sky-high expectations, but it was hard to disguise the glee. Gordon Brown appeared to accept that control of London had slipped from his party's grasp for the first time in a generation when he gave media interviews at Downing Street revealing that he had spoken to Ken that morning and congratulated him on his record. Elsewhere, copies of the Greater London Authority Act were being pulled out and dusted off as newsrooms started discussing how soon Ken would have to leave City Hall and at what hour – precisely – Boris would become Mayor. The same discussions were beginning to take place in the temporary media suite on the ninth floor of City Hall, in what is known as London's Living Room, usually a venue for receptions and parties, which boasts panoramic views of the capital.

There, as the sun beat down on the glass walls and as Boris's huge early lead was confirmed by later returns, both the temperature and the expectation rose rapidly.

Paddy Power, the bookmaker, announced at lunchtime that it was going to start paying out on a Boris victory, news that was splashed across the West End Final edition of the *Evening Standard*. The man himself refused to be drawn, however, when speaking to reporters as he left his home. 'I think the party's done fantastically nationally but London is a very different kettle of fish. We'll have to see what happens,' was all he would say.

At 4.30 p.m., Brian Paddick arrived at City Hall to do a round of what he described in his diary as 'pointless' media interviews. His major complaint was that the media had been 'unfair and biased' in its reporting of the race, making it 'very difficult to get fair and reasonable coverage' for his own campaign. 'People ask me if I have enjoyed the campaign and I say "now and again",' he lamented, although his campaign team believed he had performed creditably and hoped that the Liberal Democrats could still make gains in the Assembly.

Half an hour later Labour tossed its first bone to the media pack in the form of a calm, but suitably contrite-looking, Tessa Jowell. As the Minister for London spoke to Carolyn Quinn for Radio 4's *PM* programme, she was surrounded. Jowell declared herself 'very sorry' about the hundreds of Labour councillors who had lost their seats. But the Labour Party was not dying, she insisted, and Brown would listen to what the voters had said and act on it. But she did become the first Labour minister, and certainly the first campaign insider, to publicly follow Brown's lead and acknowledge – even if still only implicitly – that Ken had indeed lost.

As the afternoon turned into evening, and as the figures from the three counting centres began to firm up, it became clear that Boris was maintaining his lead. Although precise numbers were not being given out, the bar charts on screens around City Hall showing how the votes were accumulating as the counts progressed gave Boris the lead in eight of the fourteen GLA constituencies – and by a large margin in those (Conservative) areas with the highest turnouts. A special late edition of the *Evening Standard* was printed, declaring 'Boris is the Mayor', although the media pack was beginning to get uppity about when that would become official, since deadlines for the following day's first editions were fast approaching. It was increasingly evident that the initial estimated declaration time of 8.30 p.m. had slipped, not least because the turnout – by then confirmed as around 45 per cent of the eligible electorate – was much higher than at the previous two mayoral elections. Prior to the count, it had been suggested that the first results from the Assembly constituencies would emerge towards the end of the afternoon, but in the event the first seat did not declare until shortly before 9 p.m. Journalists from the 24-hour news channels were regularly popping up on television screens around the world but with very little new to add, whilst radio programmes being broadcast live to the nation had to fill the airwaves for far more hours than had been anticipated. But the wait continued and the frustration of the journalists in the media centre was only compounded when the stall selling overpriced refreshments closed for the evening. Journalists and commentators gravitated from one makeshift studio to the next, speculating about the result and its implications for the parties, their leaders and London itself. Among the pundits proving popular turns on the air were Andrew Hosken and Andrew Gimson, the biographers of Ken and Boris respectively, Andrew Gilligan of the *Evening Standard* and Tony Travers, a London government expert from the London School of Economics. Mark Perry from the BBC's *Dead Ringers* even popped up to amuse audiences with his impersonations of the two mayoral frontrunners.

Newsnight – which had expected to be analysing the result of the mayoral election – came and went on BBC Two, as an increasingly weary Jowell finally admitted her fear that Ken had lost.

At about 11.30 p.m., the call went up for the mayoral candidates and their agents to meet the returning officer – the sign that a declaration was imminent. In City Hall, the Assembly Chamber quickly began to fill up: with journalists, who packed into lifts taking them from the ninth to the second floor, and with the candidates' campaign teams, family and supporters, who had been milling around in the building's café on the lower ground floor and in rooms allocated to each party. Ken was thought to have been in the building all day, latterly anticipating clearing his desk, whilst Boris had turned up only shortly before the result was expected.

It was not until 11.54 p.m. – nearly forty-one hours after polling stations had opened and almost twenty-six after they had closed – that the returning officer, Anthony Mayer, delivered the voters' verdict. On the first count alone, Boris had secured in excess of one million votes – 1,043,761 to be precise – with Ken trailing in second place on 893,877, which itself was an increase of more than 200,000 on his performance in 2004. Paddick was squeezed into a poor third with less than 10 per cent of the vote. Boris and Ken had secured 43.2 and 37.0 per cent of the vote respectively, meaning that second-preference votes would have to be taken into consideration. Yet Boris's 6-point lead after the first count remained intact as valid second preferences from the other eight candidates transferred almost equally between the two frontrunners. Boris picked up a further 124,977 votes to Ken's 135,089, giving final tallies of 1,168,738 (53.2 per cent) and 1,028,966 (46.8 per cent) – the exact result predicted by the eve-of-poll YouGov survey for the *Evening Standard*.

Boris, watched by his wife and four children, went straight to the podium as London's Mayor-elect to deliver a gracious victory speech, which was far from triumphalist and extremely generous to his defeated opponents. After thanking his family, his supporters and various of the also-rans (although not the British National Party candidate, Richard Barnbrook) he paid tribute to his 'two colleagues in the strange triumvirate who have been trundling around London's church halls and TV studios violently disputing the meaning of multiculturalism and the exact cost of [bus] conductors'. He commended Paddick's 'common sense and decency' and hinted that he would like to benefit from his advice on policing matters. But he reserved his warmest words for the man whom he had just put out of a job. Describing Ken as 'a very considerable public servant and a distinguished leader of this city', he congratulated him on having shaped the office of London Mayor and for having spoken for the capital after the terrorist attacks on 7 July 2005. 'I can tell you that your courage and the sheer exuberant nerve with which you stuck it to your enemies, especially in New Labour, you have thereby earned the thanks and admiration of millions of Londoners, even if you think that they have a funny way of showing it today,' he said. Perhaps most surprising after this famous victory was Boris's assertion that 'I do not for one minute believe that this election shows that London has been transformed overnight into a Conservative city'. Signalling a desire to run an inclusive administration, he asked all those who love London to 'put aside party differences' to try and make the city even greater, although he did say that he hoped the result showed that the Conservatives had changed into a party that could again be trusted with power. He promised to work 'flat out' to earn the trust of those who hadn't supported him and to justify the confidence of those who had – even if, he admitted, many had let the pencil hover over his box before doing so. The new Mayor finished by quoting a series of phrases in the format adapted from the prayer of St Francis of Assisi, just as Margaret Thatcher had done on entering Downing Street in

1979. 'Where there have been mistakes, we will rectify them. Where there are achievements, we will build on them. Where there are neglected opportunities, we will seize on them,' he said, before concluding: 'Let's get cracking tomorrow and let's have a drink tonight.' For a man who had been off alcohol throughout the campaign, that drink must have been particularly sweet.

Ken was equally gracious at a moment when he could have blamed his demise on the performance of the Labour Government nationally or the *Evening Standard*, to name just two factors which created what one of his advisers dubbed the political 'perfect storm' and doubtless contributed to his defeat. But instead, in an emotional speech, he took it on the chin and blamed himself. 'I'm sorry I couldn't get an extra few points that would take us to victory and the fault for that is solely my own. You can't be Mayor for eight years and then if you don't get a third term say it was somebody else's fault. I accept that responsibility,' he said. The party which had once expelled him, only to take him back with gritted teeth, was subject to a warm tribute: 'The Labour Party came together in an amazing and disciplined way. There is absolutely nothing that I could have asked from the Labour Party that it didn't throw into this election, from Gordon Brown right the way down to the newest recruit handing out leaflets on very wet, cold days,' he said. And Ken too was far from partisan in his concluding remarks. 'Boris, the next few years will be the best few years of your life. This is the most amazing city to be elected Mayor and I really give you my assurance to do all I can to help the new administration in any way it seeks, but in whatever role, I will continue whilst I live in this city to love this city and to work to make it better.'

The only note of controversy came after Brian Paddick and Siân Berry, placed third and fourth respectively, had said their piece. Before Richard Barnbrook, the fifth-placed BNP candidate, could reach the podium, Livingstone, Johnson, Paddick and Berry pointedly left the stage. Watched by BNP leader Nick Griffin and a small band of supporters, Barnbrook proceeded to deliver a tirade against the political establishment, subject to heckling from some of the few audience members who chose to remain in the chamber.

David Cameron was among the first to hail his old friend's victory, which was the icing on the cake for him after the previous day's Conservative performance in the local elections. Boris signalled his intention to stand down as MP for Henley 'as soon as possible', which would create a safe berth for a Conservative candidate to take on at a by-election. In a post-victory interview, Boris insisted that there was no discontinuity between the 'Old Boris' of *Have I Got News for You* and the 'New Boris' who now had the largest single mandate of any elected politician in Britain. 'I was elected as New Boris and I will govern as New Boris, or whatever the phrase is,' he joked – in a rather Old Boris kind of way. He then headed for the Conservative Party's campaign headquarters at Millbank Tower in Westminster where a party was in full swing, although he had to break from celebrations momentarily to take a call of congratulations from Michael Bloomberg, the Mayor of New York, who would repeat his good wishes during a visit to London a week later.

Back at City Hall, however, there was still the outstanding matter of announcing the results of the election to the London Assembly. The fourteen constituency results had trickled in between 9 p.m. and 11 p.m., with the Conservatives taking eight seats to Labour's six – including a Labour gain from the Conservatives in Brent & Harrow, which includes Ken's own backyard. And whilst the Conservative majorities significantly increased in their safest seats, such as Bexley & Bromley, Havering & Redbridge and West Central, they also failed to win Enfield & Haringey, the one seat they had had high hopes of snatching from Labour. Also buoyed by a relatively good turnout of its core supporters in its strongest areas, Labour saw increases in its Assembly members' majorities in seats such as City & East and Lambeth & Southwark. Meanwhile, Liberal Democrat hopes of gaining the South West seat from the Conservatives failed to materialise.

When the result of the London-wide vote for the party lists was announced around 1 a.m., it was clear that neither of the two main parties had managed to capture as many votes as their mayoral candidates, although the Conservative and Labour vote shares of 34.6 per cent and 27.6 per cent were both up on the performance of four years previously. After the party unexpectedly lost Brent & Harrow, the Conservatives became eligible for three top-up seats, giving them a net gain of two seats on their 2004 performance. So unexpected had this been that the beneficiary of this third top-up seat, Gareth Bacon, had gone to bed and was woken by a phone call at 1 a.m. telling him about his new job. With the heightened turnout Labour actually managed a net gain of one seat. The Liberal Democrats, by contrast, had a terrible night. Although they secured more actual votes than Paddick had managed to attract, the squeeze they suffered in the mayoral contest was mirrored in the Assembly voting, where they trailed a poor third on 11.4 per cent of the vote – meaning that they lost two of their five Assembly seats. The Greens, on 8.4 per cent, retained their two existing seats, whilst the twenty-fifth member of the Assembly would be Barnbrook, after the BNP narrowly broke the 5 per cent threshold required to gain representation.

The following day, Saturday, the newly elected Mayor temporarily swapped his bike for a taxi and headed straight back to City Hall, where he was sworn into office. He arrived to a standing ovation from around 400 supporters, who chanted his name and offered him rapturous applause. After signing the declaration officially to accept the job, he immediately reasserted his manifesto pledge to make tackling crime his priority in office. This was all the more poignant since Lyle

Tulloch, a fifteen-year-old boy from Peckham, had been stabbed in a block of flats in Borough in the early hours of the morning, just as the Tories had been toasting Boris's election victory. Describing the death as tragic, he said that 'this problem of kids growing up without boundaries and getting lost in tragic and self-destructive choices is the number one issue we face in this city. It is the job of me as Mayor to lead the fightback against it.'

He also reiterated his intention to reform and improve the congestion charge and to tackle disorder on public transport. And there was more of the inclusive tone from the night before when he said that he wanted people to 'put aside any personal rancour or ideological disputes … and work together and build on the very considerable achievements of the last Mayor of London'. Yet there were touches of Old Boris too. He had needed to ask what the date was when he signed the acceptance document and managed to trip as he stepped up to make his speech from a podium. There was a typically Johnsonian turn of phrase during the speech when he warned that he would have no truck with anyone who begrudged the change of administration. 'If there are any dogs in the manger, I will have those dogs humanely euthanased,' he said. He noted the fact that it would not be until midnight the following day that he would actually receive the seals of office after Ken had cleared his desk. 'Until that time, I imagine there are shredding machines quietly puffing and panting away in various parts of the building, and quite right too,' he joked. 'Heaven knows what we shall uncover in the course of the next few days.' And with that, he headed for private meetings with the Commissioner and Deputy Commissioner of the Metropolitan Police, Sir Ian Blair and Paul Stephenson, and Transport Commissioner Peter Hendy, in order to begin discussing the implementation of his manifesto.

Next morning, the Sunday papers included much speculation

about what the Boris mayoralty would entail. It was clear that among his earliest priorities would be recruiting 440 new police community support officers to patrol public transport, increasing security at railway stations, setting up an inquiry into waste at City Hall, consulting afresh on the western extension of the congestion charge zone, and banning alcohol on the Tube and buses. His first official engagement as Mayor that Sunday was to attend a busy event in Trafalgar Square marking the Sikh festival of Vaisakhi, where he was warmly received and attracted large numbers of well-wishers. And as if to emphasise his intention to prioritise crime as an issue, he even posed for photographs wearing a policeman's hat. 'The last few days have been very, very exciting and very, very exhausting, but this is the single most wonderful job in British politics,' he concluded.

A fascinating new chapter in London politics had just begun.

Epilogue

In his first weeks in office Boris Johnson has made his key appointments and has set a very clear direction for his administration. And whilst he remains a slightly unknown quantity in this role, these steps both give some indication of what Mayor Boris will mean for London, and for the country, over the next four years.

The people are key. First was Ray Lewis, from Eastside Young Leaders Academy, appointed Deputy Mayor for Young People. Lewis is a passionate believer in the power of the voluntary sector to achieve change which government sometimes seems powerless to effect. The appointment reflected Boris's campaign, which had focused on tackling deprivation, social exclusion and poverty of ambition among young people as a way of dealing with problems of crime and anti-social behaviour more broadly. But it also reflected a change in Boris during the campaign, which he says had 'a profound effect on my whole approach to politics'. 'People's preoccupations are very similar' in Henley and parts of inner London, he said, but 'the scale of the problem is much bigger' than he had realised. Being MP for a comfortable Oxfordshire seat had insulated him from 'really having to deal with issues that relate to modern Britain'. This – tackling deprivation and inequality – will be 'a huge part of what we do in the next four years'.

The evident passion for and growing awareness of this issue mirrors the personal journey of the former Conservative leader Iain Duncan Smith, who has made tackling what he calls 'breakdown Britain' his political mission. Boris talks, too, in terms rather similar to David Cameron about how 'the rich have a duty to the poor – we all have a duty to each other'. This mood has infected the whole Conservative Party, which is committed to the kind of voluntary sector solutions which Lewis will now promote in London. In this area, as in several others, City Hall will now be a kind of laboratory for Conservative ideas. Boris doesn't like the term, but does accept that this is a chance to 'show what Compassionate Conservatism really means'. It demonstrates, he says, that the Conservatives are 'at long last engaging with issues that really matter in this country', in the cities as well as in the countryside.

If Lewis was the appointment which said most about Boris's policy priorities, the most significant in terms of governance was Tim Parker. Parker will be First Deputy Mayor, chief executive of the GLA Group* and chairman of Transport for London. He will act as chief executive of Boris's empire whilst the Mayor acts as chairman. Parker's role will be implementing Boris's vision and making sure it is done efficiently and effectively – 'value for money' is a key phrase for the new administration. Parker, who will take a nominal salary of just £1, has a record of turning around failing companies and Boris clearly hopes he will do the same, possibly involving the same remedies, at City Hall. Those remedies will not always be popular: the unions gave him the nickname 'the Prince of Darkness' on account of his job-slashing in previous lives at Clarks, the AA and Kwik-Fit.

Parker was joined by other private sector talent, including Harvey

* The GLA Group comprises the Greater London Authority, Transport for London, the Metropolitan Police Authority, the London Development Agency and the London Fire and Emergency Planning Authority.

McGrath and Peter Rogers at the London Development Agency, Carphone Warehouse's co-founder David Ross on the 2012 Olympic board, and Barclays boss Bob Diamond in charge of the Mayor's Fund. Many of the other new faces are from London Conservative circles – Ian Clement, who stood down as Leader of Bexley Council to become Deputy Mayor for Government Relations; Assembly member Kit Malthouse, Deputy Mayor for Policing; Sir Simon Milton, the leader of Westminster Council, who became senior adviser on planning, and the leader of the Conservative group on the Assembly, Richard Barnes, was appointed Statutory Deputy Mayor. Kulveer Ranger, a transport consultant and former Conservative Party vice-chairman, became director for transport policy, and Boris appointed Steve Norris to the boards of both TfL and the LDA. Guto Harri, the former BBC political correspondent who was a contemporary of Boris's at Oxford, joined as director of communications. The other significant appointees in the first batch were the Labour MP for Vauxhall, Kate Hoey, as sport commissioner (promised during the last week of the campaign), and Munira Mirza as director of policy for arts, culture and the creative industries.

Several senior City Hall figures from Ken's era went in the other direction, including Anthony Mayer, the GLA chief executive, Manny Lewis, the chief executive of the LDA, the LDA chair, Mary Reilly, and Dave Wetzel from the board of TfL. Intriguingly Neale Coleman, one of Ken's inner team, is to stay on as the GLA adviser on the London Olympics.

During the campaign Boris was very critical of Ken's sometimes antagonistic approach as Mayor, and he promised to adopt a more conciliatory style. Once in office, the first to feel the benefits of the new approach was Thames Water: Boris did an early deal with them to leave fewer unattended roadworks and introduce new water-saving schemes; in exchange he ended Ken's legal action against their planned desalination plant in Beckton. He also reached a deal with First Great Western to fully 'Oysterise' their London stations. But the main beneficiaries of the new approach should be the London boroughs, often the object of Ken's scorn when they crossed swords. Boris says that he will need the boroughs' co-operation to get several of his schemes off the ground – Westminster Council owns most of the land needed for his proposed bicycle hire scheme, for example. But the Mayor obviously has a very different remit to the boroughs – with a London-wide strategic view his interests are sometimes bound to clash with theirs. With so many local government figures on his team, will he be able to take the fight to them where necessary? Boris insists he will not be afraid to use a bit of 'mayoral fist in velvet glove'. He will be, he says, 'forceful, very forceful, where it really matters to London'. He even says he sometimes admired Ken's aggression, pressing on to get things done even when he took a lot of flak.

It isn't the only expression of admiration, and after months on the campaign trail together there seems to be a real warmth between the outgoing and incoming Mayors. Boris grew to like and admire Ken for his interest in history and ideas. 'I like him very much,' he says, and hopes they will get together for a drink in the first few weeks of his mayoralty. That has not stopped him keeping campaign commitments to abolish parts of Ken's infrastructure. Gone is the oil-for-advice deal with Venezuela (instead there is a new 'partnership and exchange programme' with New York). Gone too is the *Londoner* newspaper, and Boris has already planted the first of the 10,000 trees to be funded by its abolition. On their way out are booze on the Tube and the half-yearly black cab inspections. In halfway houses are crime mapping, which has run into some trouble with the Information Commissioner, and the 'Kenbassies' as Boris considers their role and costs. Boris has also set up a panel to investigate how money is spent at the GLA and LDA and to find ways of running things more efficiently.

His victory and this early whirlwind of activity have certainly given Boris a popularity honeymoon. He can't walk through central London without people approaching and congratulating him, telling him they voted for him, asking for a picture, wishing him well, reminding him of a commitment. And whilst that is unlikely to last forever, he looks to have brought in the people and established the structures through which he hopes to deliver on the tougher commitments. He will chair both the London Waste and Recycling Board and the Metropolitan Police Authority himself, making it clear to some where his personal priorities lie. Yet he is also returning to writing regularly for the *Telegraph*, and critics will no doubt seize on that, too, as evidence of where his priorities lie.

What will his mayoralty mean for Londoners' sense of themselves? Will he continue Ken's pursuit of an identity for Londoners? Not in quite the same way, but neither will he abandon it. He has made clear that he does not see London as a discrete city state; it is 'our capital', capital of England and the UK. But he does want to unite people and emphasise what Londoners share, and there will be a formal 'Convention on London' to agree what that is. He says London mustn't end up in a few years with the problems of social dislocation and rioting which Paris has with its suburbs; he wants to be the Mayor who deals with underachievement in the inner London boroughs. And whilst he accepts that the Mayor can't do it alone – he will need the help and support of national government – he sees his job as setting out what there is to do, articulating the challenge. As a spokesman and voice for London he will be following in Ken's footsteps; if he does his job successfully, and his team of experts begins to get a grip on the city's problems, London will be in for a very exciting four years.

Appendix

Mayoral results

Final result

Candidate	Party	1st-choice votes	2nd-choice votes*	Total votes
Boris Johnson	Conservative	1,043,761	124,977	1,168,738
Ken Livingstone	Labour	893,877	135,089	1,028,966

* On papers where the 1st- and 2nd-choice votes are for the top two candidates, the 2nd-choice votes are not counted.

Results by candidate: first choices

Candidate	Party	1st-choice votes	1st-choice %	2nd-choice votes	2nd-choice %
Boris Johnson	Conservative	1,043,761	43.20	257,792	12.86
Ken Livingstone	Labour	893,877	37.00	303,198	15.13
Brian Paddick	Lib Dem	236,685	9.80	641,412	32.01
Siân Berry	Green	77,374	3.20	331,727	16.55
Richard Barnbrook	BNP	69,710	2.89	128,609	6.42
Alan Craig	CPA	39,249	1.62	80,140	4.00
Gerard Batten	UKIP	22,422	0.93	113,651	5.67
Lindsey German	Left List	16,796	0.70	35,057	1.75
Matt O'Connor	Eng Dem	10,695	0.44	73,538	3.67
Winston McKenzie	Independent	5,389	0.22	38,954	1.94

Origin of second-choice votes

To Boris

Candidate	Party	Votes
Brian Paddick	Liberal Democrats	70,157
Richard Barnbrook	British National Party	22,200
Siân Berry	Green Party	10,984
Alan Craig	Christian Peoples Alliance	10,328
Gerard Batten	UK Independence Party	6,671
Matt O'Connor	English Democrats	2,485
Lindsey German	Left List	1,327
Winston McKenzie	Independent	825

To Ken

Candidate	Party	Votes
Brian Paddick	Liberal Democrats	73,612
Siân Berry	Green Party	36,365
Alan Craig	Christian Peoples Alliance	10,352
Lindsey German	Left List	6,661
Richard Barnbrook	British National Party	4,353
Gerard Batten	UK Independence Party	1,681
Matt O'Connor	English Democrats	1,120
Winston McKenzie	Independent	945

Turnout and technical information

Areas counted	Votes
Electorate	5,419,913
Papers counted/turnout	2,456,990
Turnout %	45.33%
Change from 2004	up 8.38 points (22.67%)
Good votes:	
1st choice	2,415,958
2nd choice	2,004,078
Rejected votes:*	
1st choice	41,032
2nd choice	412,054
Rejected-vote totals include:	
Blank (no votes cast)[†]	13,034
No 2nd choice[‡]	407,840

* 'Rejected votes' refers to ballot papers where the vote has not been counted because the ballot paper has not been completed correctly. This may be because the voter has marked more than one choice in one column, because the voter identified themselves on the ballot paper, because the voter's intention is unclear or because the voter has spoiled the paper in some way.

† 'Blank (no votes cast)' refers to ballot papers where neither first nor second choice has been marked, and no vote has been counted.

‡ 'No 2nd choice' refers to ballot papers where voters have made only a first-choice vote, not a second. The first-choice vote has been counted.

London Assembly results

Final result

Party	Seats	Gain/Loss
Conservative Party	11	+2
Labour Party	8	+1
Liberal Democrats	3	-2
Green Party	2	0
British National Party	1	+1

London-wide members

Party	Votes	% vote	Change from 2004	Members elected	Change from 2004
Conservative Party	835,535	34.63	+6.79	3	+3
Liberal Democrats	275,272	11.41	-5.09	3	-2
Labour Party	665,443	27.58	+3.15	2	0
Green Party	203,465	8.43	+0.06	2	0
British National Party	130,714	5.42	+0.71	1	1
Christian Choice	70,294	2.91	n/a	0	n/a
Abolish Congestion Charge	63,596	2.64	n/a	0	n/a
Respect (G. Galloway)	59,721	2.48	-2.09	0	0
UK Independence Party	46,617	1.93	-6.25	0	0
English Democrats	25,569	1.06	n/a	0	n/a
Left List	22,583	094	n/a	0	n/a
Unity for Peace & Socialism	6,394	0.27	n/a	0	n/a
Independent (R. Alagaratnam)	3,974	0.16	n/a	0	n/a
One London	3,430	0.14	n/a	0	n/a

Constituency results

London overall

Party	2000	2004	2008
Conservative Party	33.2%	31.2%	37.4%
Labour Party	31.6%	24.7%	28.0%
Liberal Democrats	18.9%	18.4%	13.7%
Green Party	10.2%	7.7%	8.1%
UK Independence Party	0.1%	10.0%	3.0%
Christian Peoples Alliance	n/a	2.4%	2.7%
Respect	n/a	4.6%	1.1%
British National Party	n/a	n/a	0.7%
Others	5.9%	1.1%	5.2%

Barnet & Camden

Candidate	Party	Votes
Brian Coleman	Conservative Party	72,659
Nicky Gavron	Labour Party	52,966
Nick Russell	Liberal Democrats	22,213
Miranda Dunn	Green Party	16,782
Magnus Nielsen	UK Independence Party	3,678
Clement Adebayo	Christian Peoples Alliance/Christian Party	3,536
David Stevens	English Democrats	2,146
Dave Hoefling	Left List	2,074
Graham Dare	Veritas	510

Bexley & Bromley

Candidate	Party	Votes
James Cleverly	Conservative Party	105,162
Alex Heslop	Labour Party	29,925
Tom Papworth	Liberal Democrats	21,244
Paul Winnett	National Front	11,288
Ann Garrett	Green Party	9,261
Mick Greenhough	UK Independence Party	8,021
John Hemming-Clark	Independents to Save Queen Mary's Hospital	6,684
Miranda Suit	Christian Peoples Alliance/Christian Party	4,408
Steven Uncles	English Democrats	2,907
David Davis	Left List	1,050

Brent & Harrow

Candidate	Party	Votes
Navin Shah	Labour Party	57,716
Bob Blackman	Conservative Party	56,067
James Allie	Liberal Democrats	19,299
Shahrar Ali	Green Party	10,129
Zena Sherman	Christian Peoples Alliance/Christian Party	4,180
Sunita Webb	UK Independence Party	3,021
Pat McManus	Left List	2,287
Arvind Taylor	English Democrats	2,150

City & East (Barking & Dagenham, City, Newham, Tower Hamlets)

Candidate	Party	Votes
John Biggs	Labour Party	63,635
Philip Briscoe	Conservative Party	32,082
Hanif Abdulmuhit	Respect (George Galloway)	26,760
Robert Bailey	British National Party	18,020
Rajonuddin Jalal	Liberal Democrats	13,724
Heather Finlay	Green Party	11,478
Thomas Conquest	Christian Peoples Alliance/Christian Party	7,306
Michael McGough	UK Independence Party	3,078
Graham Kemp	National Front	2,350
Michael Gavan	Left List	2,274
John Griffiths	English Democrats	2,048
Julie Crawford	Independent	701

Croydon & Sutton

Candidate	Party	Votes
Stephen O'Connell	Conservative Party	76,477
Shafi Khan	Labour Party	33,812
Abigail Lock	Liberal Democrats	32,335
David Pickles	UK Independence Party	9,440
Shasha Khan	Green Party	8,969
David Campanale	Christian Peoples Alliance/Christian Party	6,910
Richard Castle	English Democrats	4,186
Zana Hussain	Left List	1,361

Ealing & Hillingdon

Candidate	Party	Votes
Richard Barnes	Conservative Party	74,710
Ranjit Dheer	Labour Party	46,072
Nigel Bakhai	Liberal Democrats	18,004
Sarah Edwards	Green Party	12,606
Ian Edward	National Front	7,939
Mary Boyle	Christian Peoples Alliance/Christian Party	5,100
Lynnda Robson	UK Independence Party	4,465
Salvinder Dhillon	Left List	2,390
Sati Chaggar	English Democrats	1,853

Enfield & Haringey

Candidate	Party	Votes
Joanne McCartney	Labour Party	52,665
Matthew Laban	Conservative Party	51,263
Monica Whyte	Liberal Democrats	23,550
Pete McAskie	Green Party	12,473
Segun Johnson	Christian Peoples Alliance/Christian Party	5,779
Sait Akgul	Left List	5,639
Brian Hall	UK Independence Party	4,682
Teresa Cannon	English Democrats	2,282

Greenwich & Lewisham

Candidate	Party	Votes
Len Duvall	Labour Party	53,174
Andy Jennings	Conservative Party	37,040
Brian Robson	Liberal Democrats	18,174
Susan Luxton	Green Party	15,607
Tess Culnane	National Front	8,509
Stephen Hammond	Christian Peoples Alliance/Christian Party	5,079
Arnold Tarling	UK Independence Party	3,910
Jennifer Jones	Left List	2,045
Johanna Munilla	English Democrats	1,716
Chris Flood	Socialist Alternative	1,587

Havering & Redbridge

Candidate	Party	Votes
Roger Evans	Conservative Party	78,493
Balvinder Saund	Labour Party	35,468
Farrukh Islam	Liberal Democrats	12,443
Lawrence Webb	UK Independence Party	12,203
Ashley Gunstock	Green Party	9,126
Leo Brookes	English Democrats	6,487
Paula Warren	Christian Peoples Alliance/Christian Party	5,533
Peter Thorogood	Independent	3,450
Carole Vincent	Left List	1,473

Lambeth & Southwark

Candidate	Party	Votes
Valerie Shawcross	Labour Party	60,601
Caroline Pidgeon	Liberal Democrats	36,953
Shirley Houghton	Conservative Party	32,835
Shane Collins	Green Party	18,011
Geoffrey Macharia	Christian Peoples Alliance/Christian Party	4,432
Jens Winton	UK Independence Party	3,012
Katt Young	Left List	1,956
Janus Polenceus	English Democrats	1,867
Jasmijn De Boo	Animals Count	1,828
Daniel Lambert	Socialist Party	1,588

Merton & Wandsworth

Candidate	Party	Votes
Richard Tracey	Conservative Party	75,103
Leonie Cooper	Labour Party	48,810
Shas Sheehan	Liberal Democrats	17,187
Roy Vickery	Green Party	14,124
Strachan McDonald	UK Independence Party	4,286
Ellen Greco	Christian Peoples Alliance/Christian Party	4,053
Steve Scott	English Democrats	2,160
Kris Stewart	Left List	1,714

North East (Hackney, Islington, Waltham Forest)

Candidate	Party	Votes
Jennette Arnold	Labour Party	73,551
Alexander Ellis	Conservative Party	45,114
Meral Ece	Liberal Democrats	28,973
Aled Fisher	Green Party	25,845
Unjum Mirza	Left List	6,019
Nicholas Jones	UK Independence Party	5,349
Maxine Hargreaves	Christian Peoples Alliance/Christian Party	5,323
John Dodds	English Democrats	3,637

South West (Hounslow, Kingston, Richmond)

Candidate	Party	Votes
Tony Arbour	Conservative Party	76,913
Stephen Knight	Liberal Democrats	49,985
Ansuya Sodha	Labour Party	30,190
John Hunt	Green Party	12,774
Andrew Cripps	National Front	4,754
Peter Dul	UK Independence Party	3,779
Sue May	Christian Peoples Alliance/Christian Party	3,718
Andrew Constantine	Free England Party	2,908
Roger Cooper	English Democrats	1,874
Tansy Hoskins	Left List	1,526

West Central (Hammersmith & Fulham, Kensington & Chelsea, **Westminster**)

Candidate	Party	Votes
Kit Malthouse	Conservative Party	86,651
Murad Qureshi	Labour Party	35,270
Julia Stephenson	Green Party	16,874
Merlene Emerson	Liberal Democrats	15,934
Paul Wiffen	UK Independence Party	3,060
Alex Vaughan	English Democrats	1,858
Explo Nani-Kofi	Left List	1,630
Abby Dharamsey	Independent	962